Life-Situation
Preaching

Life-Situation
Preaching

CHARLES F. KEMP

THE BETHANY PRESS
ST. LOUIS

DEDICATED TO THE
CONGREGATION
OF THE
FIRST CHRISTIAN CHURCH
LINCOLN, NEBRASKA

Contents

8   *Contents*

*Life-Situation
Preaching*

Introduction:

Life-Situation Preaching
and Pastoral Work

John Watson (better known as Ian Maclaren) used to say, "Be kind, for everyone you meet is fighting a hard battle." Every faithful pastor knows that this is true. When a man arrives at a new church, he is given a list of names—100, 200, 500, 1,000, or more, as the case may be. This is the church roll. Thus far they are just names, but they are his responsibility. A reception is held soon after his arrival. Here he meets a long line of people and he tries desperately to put names and faces together. As the months and years go by, the pastor sees his church roll in a totally different light. It is no longer a mere list of names. Each name has meaning. Each one represents a personality with his own needs, his own problems, his own possibilities.

As he glances down the list of names, he knows that some are "spiritual veterans." The church depends upon them. They are reliable, faithful, and loyal. Some are an inspiration to know. They are thoughtful of others, mature in their outlook, sincere in character, Christian in faith and spirit. He also knows that many of the people listed here face difficult situations; some have real problems. All of them have some problems. He knows, as he looks down the list, that this one is troubled by doubt; this one is haunted by a sense

11

of guilt; this one is burdened by a feeling of failure or use-lessness. He knows that this person has a great potential for service but continues to drift; this young person is flirting with a type of life that is bound to lead to unhappiness and ruin. He knows that one name represents a family that is facing difficult circumstances. Another family is worried about a wayward son or daughter. Another family, normal and satisfactory to outward appearances, is torn by internal tension and strife. How does he know these things? He knows them because he has visited them in their homes; he has seen them in the hospitals in times of illness; many of them have come to see him in the church study or at the parsonage. They have waited to talk to him after church or have stopped him on the street. Young people have brought him their questions and their problems after a youth meeting or during a hike or at a youth conference. These are the people he sees in his congregation on Sunday morning. To preach to them from week to week is his great privilege and responsibility. It is no easy task.

About a hundred years ago Emerson wrote in his *Journal* of a congregation in a little village church in New England.

At church today I felt how unequal is the match of words against things. Cease, O thou unauthor-ized talker, to prate of consolation, resignation, and spiritual joys in neat and balanced sentences. For I know these men who sit below. Hush quickly, for care and calamity are THINGS to them. There is the shopmaker whose daughter has gone mad, and he is looking up through his spectacles to see what you have for him. Here is my friend whose scholars are leaving him and he knows not where to turn his hand next. Here is the stage driver who has jaundice and cannot get well. Here is B, who failed last year and is looking up anxiously. Speak, thing, or hold thy peace.

The hundred years that have elapsed since Emerson's day have served only to intensify the situation.

This does not mean that everyone who comes to church has a major problem. It does not mean that they all find life a burden or are neurotic or maladjusted. Far from it! Many of them are well-adjusted, triumphant, Christian personalities. It does mean, however, that there is probably no congregation in America, of any size whatever, that does not include some people who are in need of real help.

The attempt to help meet these needs from the pulpit is what we have called "life-situation" preaching, although some people may prefer another term. Henry Sloan Coffin[1] called it "pastoral preaching," although he admitted that it was a clumsy title. Some who have been active in the pastoral psychology movement have referred to "therapeutic" preaching.[2] This is suggestive and there are some ways in which worship and preaching should be therapeutic in their results, but the term "therapeutic" is a bit restrictive in its connotation. It might exclude some aspects of preaching, like instruction, interpretation, encouragement, and inspiration, that are also a part of life-situation preaching. We do not mean to get sidetracked by semantics. The name is not important. The important thing is that the people who come to our churches find help. If the minister is able to meet the life needs of these people Sunday after Sunday, he is fulfilling one of his most significant functions.

[1]Coffin, *What to Preach,* Harper and Brothers, 1926, p. 119.
[2]See Oates, *The Christian Pastor,* Westminster Press, 1951, p. 67.

There has been widespread interest in such preaching in recent years, primarily because of the pastoral psychology movement which, in turn, was due to the development of the psychological and sociological sciences about the turn of the century. Of course, there was such preaching before 1900. Men have always preached to life situations. Chalmers' famous sermon, "The Expulsive Power of a New Affection," was a life-situation sermon with definite psychological insight. Washington Gladden used to preach a series of sermons on Sunday evenings in which he discussed the religious, theological, and social problems of that day. This was a time when men were greatly disturbed about the relationship of science and religion and the higher criticism of the Bible. These services were attended by great numbers of students in Columbus. Such subjects would not attract crowds today but they were real life situations in that day. Horace Bushnell preached a series of sermons on some of life's deepest problems. He included messages on want and waste, on physical pain, on insanity, and on the mutabilities of life. This appeared as a volume entitled *The Moral Use of Dark Things*. When we go through the published sermons of men of a former generation, we find such subjects as these: Henry Ward Beecher preached on "The Moral Teachings of Suffering"; Charles Jefferson on "The Sinfulness of Worry"; Morison of Glasgow on "The Dislike of the Commonplace." All of these sermons were preached before the modern psychological emphasis but they are life-situation sermons.

We can go back much farther than these men, however. The letters of Paul were "life situation" in nature. Read the Corinthian correspondence, for example. It deals with one problem after another, specific, practical problems that were troubling the people of his day. Even the lofty thirteenth chapter of the first letter grew out of a practical problem that existed at Corinth. Is it not reasonable to assume that if Paul dealt with life situations so effectively in correspondence, he did the same in his preaching?

Jesus spoke to life situations. Much of his preaching grew directly out of a practical life situation. That certainly was true of the story of the good Samaritan and that of the prodigal son. Some of his most spiritual statments were made to meet the life problem of one man or woman, such as Nicodemus or the woman at the well.

Books on homiletics have not usually given life-situation preaching a major emphasis, and some of the older books did not mention it at all; yet such a man as Harry Emerson Fosdick said that this is the most important thing that is done in the pulpit. In 1928 he made one of the most clearcut statments that has as yet appeared as to what such preaching should be. "Start with a life issue," he said, "a real problem, personal or social, perplexing the mind or disturbing the conscience; face that problem fairly, deal with it honestly, and then throw such light on it from the spirit of Christ, that people will be able to go out able to think more clearly and live more nobly because of that sermon."[3] In more recent years such men as Luccock, Buttrick, Bowie, and McCracken have included references to this area in their discussions of preaching.[4]

---

[3]Used by permission of the author.

[4]See Luccock, *In the Minister's Workshop*, Abingdon Press, 1934, chap. VI, "Preaching to Life Situations"; Buttrick, *Jesus Came Preaching*, Harpers, 1931, chap. V, "Preaching Christ to the Individual of Today"; Bowie, *Preaching*, Abingdon Press, 1944, chap. VIII, "Relating Theology to Life"; and McCracken, *The Making of the Sermon,* Harper & Brothers, 1956, chap. III, "The Varied Character of the Sermon," section "Psychological Preaching," p. 56ff., and "Life Situation Preaching," p. 62ff.

How Pastoral Work Contributes to Preaching

Halford Luccock, comparing life-situation preaching with other types of preaching, says, "Preaching which begins with life situations and is carefully aimed at them starts with the great initial advantage that it presents something for which the need is felt."[5] It starts where people live. Such preaching must, of necessity, have a close relationship with pastoral work. A preacher cannot speak to people's needs if he does not know what their needs are. He cannot know what people's needs are if he does not spend time with them. We might say that such preaching grows out of pastoral work. Peter Ainslie said, "If in the preparation of an article or a sermon my mind did not work with ease, I would put on my hat and make a round of calls to come back with messages seething through my brain."[6] Henry Sloan Coffin advised all men to follow such a procedure. He said,

> When a minister begins a week with the feeling that he is "preached out," let him spend an afternoon . . . in going about from family to family, and asking himself: "What is the spiritual need here? What guidance or comfort or awakening or sharpening of conscience or enrichment in God ought this home or this individual receive?"[7]

The minister who is constantly among his people, visiting them and letting them come freely to him, will not lack for themes on which to preach. This does not excuse him from

---

[5]From *In the Minister's Workshop,* by Halford E. Luccock. By permission of Abingdon Press.

[6]From *Peter Ainslie, Ambassador of Good Will,* by Idleman, copyrighted 1941. Used by permission of Harper and Brothers.

[7]From *What to Preach,* by Henry Coffin, copyrighted 1926, by Harper & Brothers. Used by permission.

spending time in his study or from using his books; rather, it should send him to his books with a new sense of reality. Sir William Osler, the great physician, used to advise young men to divide their time between books and men. This is good advice for preachers as well.

Preaching is more than the presentation of a subject. It is also a relationship between pastor and people. For this reason a study of preaching can never be merely a study of sermons.[8] We shall present some outstanding sermons, both past and present, in the following section of this volume. We feel that this has value, for these sermons were well written and they have proved to be helpful. We recognize, however, that there was more than the subject matter that was involved. It was not the fact that they were well written that made them effective. Some of the people in the pews knew the man in the pulpit. He had helped them as individuals. Because of this we have included with each sermon a biographical sketch, with the hope that it will indicate something of the attitude of this man toward his people and the relationship that existed.

If the pastor is faithful to the needs of his people; if he is present in times of sickness, trouble, and sorrow; if he is understanding with those who come to him; if he is able to relieve tensions, to restore confidence, to help with human relationships; then people will listen with a new earnestness when he speaks on Sunday. People who have known a preacher also as a pastor will give a different kind of attention when he preaches.

The opposite is also true. Pastoral work that is neglected or done poorly can weaken preaching. If the preacher speaks of human needs in general but is not interested in the

[8] See Hiltner, editorial in *Pastoral Psychology,* November, 1955, pp. 9-10.

needs of the individual, if he is too busy, if he is unwilling to give the time and effort necessary to meet these needs, then his people will question what he says on Sunday, and the effect of his preaching will be weakened no matter how eloquent or scholarly it may be.

How Preaching Contributes to Pastoral Work

Preaching, in turn, can contribute much to pastoral work. Preaching can become the preparation of, or can provide the motivation for, counseling. It has been said that the test of a sermon is the number of people who want to consult the preacher in private. It is not necessarily the concern with a specific subject that serves as a preparation for counseling as much as it is the preacher's total attitude. When the people in the congregation feel that he understands them, that he accepts them, that he has a genuine interest in them and understands life, they will also feel that he is one with whom they might share their problems and their needs.

This is the preacher's great opportunity. Many people concern themselves with people's personal problems: doctors, lawyers, social workers, psychologists, marriage counselors, and others. The men in no other profession appear before the people once a week to speak to them of the issues of life. This gives the minister a chance to surround his counseling and guidance with a philosophy of life which can serve as a background for all that he does with persons, as he sees them one by one.

Some subjects may be considered more effectively in the pulpit than in the interview. As Wayne Oates has said,

> The ministry of comfort, reassurance, instruction and interpretation can often be done more powerfully through preaching than through individual counseling, because it is done in the presence of

the larger community of worshipers. Having done this, a pastor in private conference . . . can spend his time in listening to their side of the story.[9]

Through worship and preaching, a new challenge, a new vision, a new inspiration can be given that can never be accomplished in any other setting.

Not Two Tasks But One

Preaching and pastoral work are really not two tasks but one; at least they are two functions that are so closely related that they are almost inseparable. Phillips Brooks said it in his lectures on preaching given at Yale back in 1877,

> The work of the preacher and the pastor really belong together, and ought not to be separated. I believe that very strongly. . . . When you find that you can never sit down to study and write without the faces of the people, who you know need your care, looking at you from the paper; and yet you never can go out among your people without hearing your forsaken study reproaching you, and calling you home, you may come to believe that it would be good indeed if you could be one or other of two things and not both; either a preacher or a pastor, but not the two together. But I assure you you are wrong. The two things are not two, but one. . . . The preacher needs to be a pastor, that he may preach to real men. The pastor must be preacher that he may keep the dignity of his work alive. . . . Be both; for you cannot really be one unless you also are the other.[10]

---

[9]From *The Christian Pastor,* by Wayne E. Oates, copyright, 1951, by W. L. Jenkins, The Westminster Press. Used by permission.

[10]Brooks, *Lectures on Preaching,* Dutton & Co., 1877, pp. 75-77.

The important phrase in this quotation is, "The two things are not two but one." Charles Jefferson used to say, "The minister does not cease to be a pastor when he enters the pulpit, rather he takes up one of the pastor's most exacting tasks."[11] It is not a question of which is the more important, preaching or pastoral work. Both are important; both must be done well. The minister's role is one role. His task is to help people both as preacher and as pastor, for the two functions strengthen and support each other.

Person-mindedness

The chief requirement is that the minister have what R. H. Edwards has called "person-mindedness."

> Until we sense the supreme significance of persons in our world, until we get them into central focus, until they count above everything else with us, until we are, in a word, possessed by person-mindedness, we do not have the first pre-requisite for the Christian ministry.[12]

When Phillips Brooks gave his lectures on preaching he included one lecture on "The Congregation." Certainly the preacher must know the subject on which he preaches. That is taken for granted. He also must know the congregation to which he speaks. He must know them as individuals as well as a group. Dr. Albert B. Coe has written of his preparation for preaching.

> It is my custom to spend much time in the church here alone. I walk up and down the aisles. . . . I

[11]From *The Minister as Shepherd*, by Charles Jefferson, copyright 1912, Thomas Y. Crowell Company. Used by permission.
[12]From *A Person-Minded Ministry*. Used by permission of David H. Edwards.

imagine the different individuals in the pews, seeking an intimate comprehension of each one's needs and praying for the power to meet the need in a sane, intelligent, inspired way. From my pulpit I go to the street that passes the church, see the people passing—bright faces, sad faces, the man out of work. . . . There is a woman with all the lines of distress written on her face. There is a man seeking the divorce court with his heart wracked indescribably. There they go—unhappy faces, on which are written doubt and scorn and yearning. . . . All the faces reveal a hunger for reality. I reach out to all of them.[13]

When John Frederick Oberlin was carrying on his very effective ministry in the Vosges Mountains of France, he spent an hour a day in prayer for his people. During this hour he mentioned them by name, one by one. The people passed his house in silence, for they knew he was praying for them. With such "person-mindedness" in the background of one's ministry, a man will preach to real needs.

Some Warnings and Limitations

In some ways it seems presumptuous for a man even to attempt to preach on such subjects. Who is adequate to face even a few of these life problems, not to mention the complete range of them that present themselves in any community? We do not mean that any man should attempt to solve all of these problems. We do not mean that he must find in his own thought any neat or simple solution for all of life's ills. It is not his message he presents but one that is tested by the ages. He has the entire experience of the

[13]From an article in *The Congregationalist* for Feb. 19, 1931. Used by permission.

Christian tradition from which to draw. He is a representative of the church and a proclaimer of the gospel. This makes us realize why the Bible is so important. Here is the answer to some who feel that such an approach to preaching neglects or minimizes the Bible; on the contrary, it means that the preacher must return to his Bible with a new earnestness as he attempts to use it to interpret life and to give meaning to human experience. This is an opportune time to emphasize the importance of illustrations. The illustrations are what people remember. They clarify a sermon. Every preacher should have a file of stories, especially from the lives of great men and women. These have a tremendous value for they are mirrors in which we can see ourselves. They have tested these principles in the laboratory of their own experience and have proved to be "more than conquerors." The same resources that were available to them are available to the people in our congregations today.

While speaking of illustrations, it is a good time to point out that pastoral experiences should not be used as veiled illustrations in the pulpit, no matter how interesting they are or how well they fit the sermon. When we say that preaching grows out of pastoral work, we do not mean that the illustrations do. It is a violation of confidence in the first place, and it closes the door to further confidence in the second. Even to use illustrations from another community is dangerous. Someone in the congregation may say, "If he will discuss other people's problems publicly, he might also discuss mine."

There are other warnings and limitations that should be mentioned. Life-situation preaching should not be a constant repetition of problems. It is possible to preach on life situations in such a way that one raises more problems than he solves. It is possible to make people worry about things that might not otherwise exist, like some of the ads on television and radio that discuss so many symptoms they make people think they have something they do not have. We must recognize that handling a life problem inadequately can do more harm than good. It is not right to oversimplify, or to create false hopes. To raise such an issue as doubt, fear, or guilt, and then not handle it adequately is unfair. There may be people in the congregation to whom these are vital issues.

All such preaching must be based on an understanding of human nature and its behavior. It must have in the background a sound psychology. This does not mean that such preaching should include psychological terms. In fact, such terms should be avoided. A knowledge of psychology is fine, but the language of the sermon should be the language of the people.

The minister should recognize that preaching is only one method of helping people face life's problems and live the Christian life. He should not attempt to do in the pulpit what should be done only in an interview, or perhaps in a series of interviews. We said earlier that some things can be done more adequately through preaching than in any other way. This does not mean that all things can. Some problems can be dealt with only face to face, when the person has the opportunity to express himself, to ask questions, and to relieve his tensions. That is to say that preaching must be done along with pastoral work; it can never take the place of either pastoral counseling or pastoral care.

Life-situation preaching must not be the only kind of preaching that one does. Other emphases must also be made in the course of a year's preaching. The church itself must be lifted up; missions must be advanced; social issues must be faced; evangelistic, doctrinal, biblical preaching are all important. Some of these other emphases have aspects of life-situation preaching within them. Harold Ruopp has said that life-situation preaching is not so much a type of preaching as it is an approach to preaching.[14] In this respect a social, biblical, or doctrinal sermon can also be a life-situation sermon. A sermon on stewardship can be a life-situation sermon, for much can be said to show that a man's attitude toward money is his attitude toward life. In this sense a sermon on stewardship is more than a means of raising the budget; it is a real life-situation presentation, with definite psychological implications. A sermon on missions may refer to the life of David Livingstone, or some other missionary hero, in such a way that it not only advances the cause of missions but also presents life as a courageous adventure. A sermon which presents a challenge to service can do much to help a man live triumphantly; in fact, it may solve some of his problems without talking about problems at all.

One of the most significant functions of preaching is a preventive one, the developing of resources of prayer and worship and character and faith that prevents the problems from arising and which gives resources for the facing of them when they do arise. Russell Dicks, leader in the field of pastoral care, said of preaching, "The preacher's task is to bring into the lives of his people the Eternal truths. . . . The clergyman who knows human problems but does not know Eternal truth, God and the ways of God, fails in preaching."[15]

---

[14]Ruopp, "Life-Situation Preaching," *Christian Century Pulpit,* May, 1941.
[15]From *Pastoral Work and Personal Counseling,* by Russell Dicks. Copyright 1944, The Macmillan Company. Used by permission.

There Are Results

Preaching like this does produce results. A, V. G. Allen, in his *Life of Phillips Brooks,* included this letter from a man in England, a man whom Brooks had never met.

> For the last five years I may say that I have read one of your sermons every Sunday, and the help and spiritual nourishment I get from them has been a very real source of strength and happiness in my life. . . . Often have I opened a volume of your sermons in hours of despondence and gloom, when the Unseen has seemed to be the non-existent, when all high ideals were slipping away, and the actual was pressing out faith and courage; and never did the reading of your words fail to encourage and strengthen me and send me back to suffering or action with fresh force and energy.
>
> . . .

This letter was from a man who referred only to his printed sermons, but how much more it must have applied to those who heard them from Sunday to Sunday but perhaps never wrote a letter of appreciation.

Dr. Fosdick expected results. In a sermon on the subject, "Getting Out of Us the Best That Is in Us," he said, "You know, that might happen here this morning. That is the kind of thing which ought to happen, not simply in psychiatrists' offices, but in a church. To my certain knowledge that has happened here more than once."[16] Speaking of the relationship of preaching and counseling, and referring to the fact that real changes do take place, he said,

[16]From *Hope of the World,* by Harry Emerson Fosdick, copyrighted 1933, by Harper & Brothers. Used by permission.

"Nothing so much as this experience, I suspect, can send a man into the pulpit, sure that preaching can be personal consultation on a group scale, and that someone's life that morning can be made over."[17]

The result may not be due to anything specific. It may be something that grows out of the preacher's own attitude of confidence, his faith in people and in God. As one man said, on leaving one of Phillips Brooks's services, ". . . he always makes me feel so strong." It may be an illustration or a statement that speaks to a particular need. A young woman who had gone through a rather difficult and trying experience said to her pastor that she had never forgotten a statement he had made in a sermon months before. It was the quoting of the old saying, "All the water in the seven seas cannot sink a ship unless it gets inside the ship." She said that she had never forgotten that statement and it seemed to sustain her and enable her to carry on. That sermon was worth while for that one quotation alone and for what it meant to that one young woman. It may not be something that happens all at once. It may be the accumulated influence of many sermons and many ideas that gradually and unconsciously begins to have an effect. Karl de Schweinitz, the social worker, in his classical little book on *The Art of Helping People Out of Trouble,* points out that people were a long time in becoming what they are, and we ought not expect sudden transformations. He said that with some it may take "months and years of effort." The preacher should be just as realistic, but he should never lose

[17]From "Personal Counseling and Preaching," by Harry Emerson Fosdick. Reprinted from the May, 1952, issue of *Pastoral Psychology.* Copyright 1952 by Pastoral Psychology Press, Great Neck, N. Y.

sight of the fact that change does take place. It may require a combination of preaching and counseling, and perhaps other things, too, but the possibilities are always there. This was the secret of Jesus. He saw people not as they were but as they could become. Those who would preach his gospel must do the same.

GUIDE FOR STUDYING A LIFE-SITUATION SERMON

The following questions are intended to help you in studying and evaluating these sermons from the standpoint of their effectiveness in meeting life situations.

Purpose: What is the author's central aim or objective in this sermon? Is it made clear to his listeners?

Relation to Life: What life situation, what problem, what area of experience is he facing? Is the problem primarily religious? psychological? personal? social? Is it common to all people? Does it apply to some special group? Does it apply to one age group more than others? Does it deal with a true life situation?

Treatment: Does he deal with the problem adequately? realistically? Does he oversimplify? or raise false hopes? Does he provide practical suggestions for solution? Does he utilize the resources of religion and the Christian faith?

Title: Does the title prepare the people for the sermon that will be presented? Is it attractive and inviting? Is it clear?

Scripture: Does he use a text? How does it relate to the subject he discusses? Does he use scripture to introduce a life situation? to interpret a life situation?

as a solution for life problems and situations? Does
he draw illustrations from biblical material? Does
he utilize the scriptural resources to fullest advantage? What passages or illustrations might he have
used that he did not?

Illustrations: Does he draw his illustrations from personal
experience? scripture? biography? literature? history? Do they clarify the subject? Are they true
to life and experience?

Relation to Pastoral Work: Does the sermon seem to grow
out of human experience? Does it express the
thought of one who knows, understands, and loves
people? Would it lead people to go to the one
who prepared and preached this sermon for personal guidance and help?

Life-Situation Sermons:
Past and Present

The specialists in homiletics like Andrew Blackwood and Halford Luccock say that one of the surest ways to improve one's preaching is to study good sermons. This is not to imply that this is the only way it can be done, but it is one effective way. Andrew Blackwood says, "At some early stage, almost every master preacher has made a study of printed sermons."[1] Halford Luccock, writing specifically on the subject of life-situation preaching, listed various resources which a minister should utilize. Among other areas of reading that he recommended he included "the study of sermons which have effectively done that sort of thing. The purpose of this, of course, will not be to use the material or to plagiarize but to learn from the workmanship."[2]

We have tried to provide some of this material on the pages that follow. We have included some sermons that were preached before the appearance of modern psychology and some that were preached since. One who would make a study of life-situation preaching should be familiar with what was done yesterday as well as with what is being done today. Some of these men of a former generation were very effective. They did not have available the resources of modern psychology but they had a wide experience in dealing

[1]Blackwood, *The Protestant Pulpit*, Abingdon-Cokesbury, 1947, p. 5.
[2]From *In the Minister's Workshop*, by Halford E. Luccock. By permission of Abingdon Press.

with people, which gave them a genuine understanding of human nature and a real insight into man's spiritual needs. The sermons are arranged roughly in the chronological order in which they were preached. We have not attempted to present a common point of view. The men whose sermons are included came from a variety of denominational backgrounds and represent different points of view and different theological positions, but in their preaching they all had one common purpose—to meet the needs of their people.

The problem in such a collection is not what sermons to include, but what sermons to leave out. Some people will wonder why there are no sermons here from Thomas Chalmers, F. W. Robertson, Henry Ward Beecher, Washington Gladden, and other giants of the past. Others will wonder why Roy Burkhart, Halford E. Luccock, and many others were not included. These men are preaching very effectively on life situations. That is true. There are limits of space. We have added one hundred sermon titles at the close of this volume. The mere reading of these titles gives some idea of the nature and extent of such preaching. We could not include them all. We do hope the ones we have included will be helpful.

Sometimes the difficulty came in making a selection from the sermons of one man. It is no easy task to choose one sermon from the published works of Bushnell or Brooks or Fosdick. We have tried to include sermons which present a variety of emphases, recognizing that there are many, many others that might just as well have been used.

We have attempted to select men who were effective not only in their homiletic methods, but men who were effective in relating preaching to pastoral work. The brief introductory statement before each sermon is for the purpose of giving something of the background of thought and experience of the man who preached the sermon.

It is hoped that these sermons will have value in themselves, but, more than this, that bringing them together in this way will be a stimulus to others, as they, too, face the needs of their people and the responsibilities of the Christian pulpit.

I

Horace Bushnell:
Preacher and Theologian

Horace Bushnell spent all of his ministry in one church, although his influence reached far beyond his local parish. He was noted both as a preacher and as a theologian. As we shall point out here, he was also a faithful pastor. His sermon, "Every Man's Life a Plan of God," has been referred to as one of the three greatest sermons in the English language.[1] President Timothy Dwight considered him the greatest of all the preachers who came to speak at Yale. William Warren Sweet, the church historian, says, "I do not believe that it is an exaggeration to say that much of the best preaching in America during the last half century, at least, has been largely dependent upon Horace Bushnell, the preacher's preacher."

His influence as a theologian was equally wide, although all of his biographers point out that he was not a professional theologian nor even a systematic one. Gaius Glenn Atkins says of Bushnell's thinking, "The age he inherited approached life through doctrine. He approached doctrine through life."[2] His volume on *Christian Nurture* shows psychological insights that were far in advance of his day. His writing was

---

[1]From *Makers of Christianity*, by William Warren Sweet, copyrighted 1937, by Henry Holt and Company, Inc. Used by permission.
[2]Atkins, *Master Sermons of the Nineteenth Century*, Willett and Clark, 1940, p. 153.

as far-reaching in its influence as that of any man of his generation. All of this is interesting as a background, but our primary interest here is in his preaching and his pastoral work and the relationship of one with the other.

Bushnell was a man of great faith. Through his preaching, his writing, and his personal counseling he was able to help many others find faith. In his own experience faith did not come easily. There was a time when as a young man he said, "My religious faith is utterly gone." It was a time when he said he experienced "agonies of mental darkness concerning God." How he worked through the problem from doubt to faith is too lengthy to record here. The important thing is that he did so and out of his own experience he was able to be of great help to others.

– Although he was noted as a theologian and was by nature a scholar, he kept in close touch with his people. He very frankly admitted that pastoral work was difficult for him, but he sensed its importance, cultivated its art, and in spite of all of his writings and other activities he never neglected it. In fact, his later letters indicate his wish that he could devote more time to it. • One reason his theology was so closely related to life was that he kept so closely related to life himself. He wanted to know all his people personally and to visit them all once a year—more frequently if the occasion demanded. •

A letter tells how he ministered to the invalid daughter of one of his parishioners. "In our times of trial and affliction, Dr. Bushnell would, if at home, be sure to be on hand; and those seasons, sometimes of long continuance, were frequent with me. My daughter, after several severe illnesses, was at last a confirmed invalid, confined to her bed for nearly nine years. When at home, he used always to call upon her once every week, usually on Monday morning. It did not seem to be possible for any man to manifest more tender sympathy and care for her spiritual interests than he did. He was always faithful, always true, to me and mine."[3]

Such an illustration is no isolated instance but an example of the faithfulness with which he cared for all of his people. He also sought to make it possible for individuals to come to him. He not only welcomed people at his home, but it was his custom for many years to spend one evening a week at his church office, where he was available to anyone who wished to consult him about any personal or religious matter. It was especially noted that many young men took advantage of this opportunity. One said it was here that he learned the meaning of religion in practical life. There was one who came to consult him every week in an attempt to overcome a quick temper. Another he helped to free from "the tyranny of a morbid conscience," and enabled him to develop courage and faith.

A friend came to him much worried about the nervous restlessness of his child. A woman came who was greatly confused about her religious beliefs. She expected an argument, but instead found one who met her with sympathy and understanding and was able to help her find faith.

Regardless of who the person might be, the seriousness of the problem, or the importance of other tasks at hand, the individual was always received with a sincere welcome, and the problem was faced with patience and understanding.

His own struggle for faith, all of his dealing with people is in the background of a sermon he preached in the chapel

[3]From *Life and Letters of Horace Bushnell*, by Mary Bushnell Cheney, copyrighted 1903 by Charles Scribner's Sons. Used by permission.

at Yale on "The Dissolving of Doubts." There are notations
in the manuscript which indicate where he departed from
the prepared presentation to refer to his own experience.
Here he deals with a problem that must be faced anew in
each generation.

THE DISSOLVING OF DOUBTS[1] *Weak*

By Horace Bushnell

*"And I have heard of thee, that thou canst
make interpretations and dissolve doubts."*
—Dan. 5:16.

Doubts and questions are not peculiar to Nebuchadnezzar,
but they are the common lot and heritage of humanity.
They vary in their subjects and times, but we have them
always on hand. We live just now in a specially doubting
age, where almost every matter of feeling is openly doubted,
or, it may be, openly denied. Science puts every thing in
question, and literature distils the questions, making an
atmosphere of them. We doubt both creation and Creator;
whether there be second causes or only primal causes running *ab æterno* in *æternum;* whether God is anything more
than the sum of such causes; whether he works by will back
of such causes; whether he is spirit working supernaturally
through them; whether we have any personal relation to
him, or he to us. And then, when we come to the matter
of revelation, we question the fact of miracles and of the
incarnation. We doubt free agency and responsibility, immortality and salvation, the utility of prayer and worship,
and even of repentance for sin. And these sweeping, deso-
lating doubts run through all grades of mind, all modes and
spheres of life, as it were telegraphically, present as powers
of the air to unchristen the new-born thoughts of religion
as fast as they arrive. The cultivated and mature have the
doubts ingrown they know not how, and the younger minds

[1]From *Sermons on Living Subjects*.

encounter their subtle visitations when they do not seek
them.   And the more active-minded they are, and the more
thoughts they have on the subject of religion, the more likely
they are, (unless anchored by true faith in God,) to be
drifted away from all the most solid and serious convictions,
even before they are aware of it.   Their mind is ingenuous,
it may be, and their habit is not over-speculative, certainly
not perversely speculative; they only have a great many
thoughts raising a great many questions that fly, as it were,
loosely across their mental landscape, and leave no trace of
their passage—that is, none which they themselves perceive,—and yet they wake up by and by, startled by the discovery that they believe nothing.   They can not any where
put down their foot and say, "here is truth."   And it is the
greatest mystery to them that they consciously have not
meant to escape from the truth, but have, in a certain sense,
been feeling after it.   They have not been ingenious in their
questions and arguments.   They have despised all tricks of
sophistry, they have only been thinking and questioning as
it seemed to be quite right they should.   And yet, somehow,
it is now become as if all truth were gone out, and night and
nowhere had the world.   The vacuity is painful, and they
are turned to a wrestling with their doubts, which is only
the more painful that they wrestle, as it were, in mid-air,
unable to so much as touch ground anywhere.

The point I am sketching here is certainly in the extreme,
and yet it is an extreme often reached quite early, and one
toward which all young minds gravitate, as certainly as they
consent to live without God and carry on their experience,
steadied by no help from the practical trust of religion.
Probably some of you, my friends here before me, are at
one point of doubt or unbelieving, and some at another; I

sincerely hope that none of you have reached the dark extreme just described. But whatever point you have reached, I propose for my object this morning to bring in what I can of countervailing help. I shall speak of the dissolving of your doubts, showing how you may have them dissolved in all their degrees and combinations. If they do not press you, or at all trouble you; if you like to have them, and amuse yourself in what you count the brilliancy of their play, if you love to be inventive and propagate as many and plausible as you may, I have nothing for you. But if you want to know the truth—all truth—and be in it, and have all the fogs of the mind cleared away, I think I can tell you in what manner it may, without a peradventure, be done. Shall I go on? Give me then your attention, nothing more. I shall not ask you to surrender up your will or suppress your intelligence, would not even consent to have you force your convictions or opinions. All that I ask is a real desire to find the truth and be in it.

Before proceeding, however, in the principal matter of the subject, it may be well to just note the three principal sources and causes whence our doubts arise, and from which they get force to make their assault. They never come of truth or high discovery, but always of the want of it.

In the first place, all the truths of religion are inherently dubitable. They are only what are called probable, never necessary truths like the truths of geometry or of numbers. In these we have the premises in our very minds themselves. In all other matters we have the premise to find. And there is almost no premise out of us that we do not some time or other doubt. We even doubt our senses, nay, it takes a very dull, loose-minded soul, never to have, or to have had a doubt of the senses. Now this field of probable truth is the whole field of religion, and of course it is competent for doubt to cover it in every part and item.

In the second place, we begin life as unknowing creatures that have every thing to learn. We grope, and groping is doubt; we handle, we question, we guess, we experiment, beginning in darkness and stumbling on towards intelligence. We are in a doom of activity, and can not stop thinking— thinking every thing, knocking against the walls on every side; trying thus to master the problems, and about as often getting mastered by them. Yeast works in bread scarcely more blindly. When I draw out this whole conception of our life as it is, the principal wonder, I confess, is that we doubt so little and accept so much.

And, again, thirdly, it is a fact, disguise it as we can, or deny it as we may, that our faculty is itself in disorder. A broken or bent telescope will not see any thing rightly. A filthy window will not bring in even the day as it is. So a mind wrenched from its true lines of action or straight perception, discolored and smirched by evil, will not see truly, but will put a blurred, misshapen look on every thing. Truths will only be as good as errors, and doubts as natural as they.

Now it will be seen that as long as these three sources or originating causes of doubt continue, doubts will continue, and will, in one form or another, be multiplied. Therefore, I did not propose to show how they may be stopped, for that is impossible, but only how they may be dissolved, or cleared away. I may add, however, that the method by which they are to be dissolved, will work as well preventively as remedially; for though it will not stop their coming, it will stop their coming with damage and trouble to the mind, and keep it clear for all steadiest repose and highest faith in religion.

And the first thing here to be said, and it may be most important, is negative; viz., that the doubters never can dissolve or extirpate their doubts by inquiry, search, investigation, or any kind of speculative endeavor. They must never go after the truth to merely find it, but to practice it and live by it. It is not enough to rally their inventiveness, doing nothing to polarize their aim. To be simply curious, thinking of this and thinking of that, is only a way to multiply doubts; for in doing it they are, in fact, postponing all the practical rights of truth. They imagine, it may be, that they are going first, to settle their questions, and then, at their leisure, to act. As if they were going to get the perfect system and complete knowledge of truth before they move an inch in doing what they know! The result is that the chamber of their brain is filled with an immense clatter of opinions, questions, arguments, that even confound their reason itself. And they come out wondering at the discovery, that the more they investigate the less they believe! Their very endeavor mocks them,—just as it really ought. For truth is something to be lived, else it might as well not be. And how shall a mind get on finding more truth, save as it takes direction from what it gets; how make farther advances when it tramples what it has by neglect? You come upon the hither side of a vast intricate forest region, and your problem is to find your way through it. Will you stand there inquiring and speculating forty years, expecting first to make out the way? or, seeing a few rods into it, will you go on as far as you see, and so get ability to see a few rods farther? proceeding in that manner to find out the unknown, by advancing practically in the known.

No, there is no fit search after truth which does not, first of all, begin to live the truth it knows. Alas! to honor a little truth is not in the doubters, or they do not think of it, and so they dishonor beforehand all the truth they seek, and swamp it, by inevitable consequence, in doubts without end.

Dropping now this negative matter, we come to the positive. There is a way for dissolving any and all doubts,—a way that opens at a very small gate, but widens wonderfully after you pass. Every human soul, at a certain first point of its religious outfit, has a key given it which is to be the *open sesame* of all right discovery. Using this key as it may be used, any lock is opened, any doubt dissolved. Thus every man acknowledges the distinction of right and wrong, feels the reality of that distinction, knows it by immediate consciousness even as he knows himself. He would not be a man without that distinction. It is even this which distinguishes him from the mere animals. Having it taken away, he would, at the same instant, drop into an animal. I do not say, observe, that every man is clear as to what particular things may be fitly called right and what wrong. There is a great disagreement here in men's notions; what is right to some, or in some ages and some parts of the world, being wrong to others, in other times and countries. I only say that the distinction of *idea* or *general principle* is the same in all ages and peoples, without a shade of difference. Their ideas of space and time are not more perfectly identical. So far they are all in the same great law; constituted, in that fact, men, moral beings, subjects of religion. Their whole nature quivers responsively to this law. To be in the right, and of it, to mean the right, and swear allegiance to it forever, regardless of cost, even though it be the cost of life itself,—they can as well disown their existence as disown this law. There may be now and then a man who contrives to raise a doubt of it, and yet, driven out with rods, it will come back, a hundred times a day, and force its recognition; especially if any one does him a wrong.

Here, then, is the key that opens every thing. And the only reason why we fall into so many doubts, and get unsettled by our inquiries, instead of being settled by them as we undertake to be, is that we do not begin at the beginning. Of what use can it be for a man to push on his inquiries after truth, when he throws away, or does not practically honor, the most fundamental and most determinating of all truths? He goes after truth as if it were coming in to be with him in wrong! even as a thief might be going after honest company in stolen garments. How can a soul, unpolarized by wrong, as a needle by heat, settle itself in the poles of truth? Or who will expect a needle, hung in a box of iron, turning every way and doubting at every point of compass, to find the true North? But a right mind has a right polarity, and discovers right things by feeling after them. Not all right things in a moment, though, potentially, all in a moment; for its very oscillations are true, feeling after only that which is, to know it as it is.

The true way, therefore, of dissolving doubts, as I just now said, is to begin at the beginning, and do the first thing first. Say nothing of investigation, till you have made sure of being grounded everlastingly, and with a completely whole intent, in the principle of right doing as a principle. And here it is, let me say, that all unreligious men are at fault, and often without knowing, or even suspecting it. They do right things enough in the out-door, market sense of the term, and count that being right. But let them ask the question, "Have I ever consented to be, and am I really

now, in the right, as in principle and supreme law; to live
for it, to make any sacrifice it will cost me, to believe everything it will bring me to see, to be a confessor of Christ as
soon as it appears to be enjoined upon me, to go on a mission
to the world's end, if due conviction sends me, to change my
occupation for good conscience' sake, to repair whatever
wrong I have done to another, to be humbled, if I should
before my worst enemy, to do complete justice to God, and,
if I could, to all worlds?—in a word, to be in wholly right
intent, and have no mind but this forever?" Ah, how soon
do they discover possibly, in this manner, that they are right
only so far as they can be, and not be at all right as in principle—right as doing some right things, nothing more. Of
course, they are not going to be martyrs in this way, and
they have not had a thought of it.

After this there is not much use in looking farther, for if
we can not settle ourselves practically in this grand first
law which we do know, how can we hope to be settled in
what of truth we do not? Are we ready, then, to undertake a matter so heavy? for the struggle it requires will be
great, as the change itself must be well nigh total; a revolution so nearly complete, that we shall want every help we
can get. And let us not be surprised by the suggestion that
God, perchance, may come to our help unseen, when we do
not so much as know how to believe in him, only let it occur
to us how great a comfort it should be, to have a God so
profoundly given to the right; for that subtle gleam of sympathy may be itself a kind of prayer,—prayer that he will
answer before the call is heard. And then, as certainly as
the new right mind begins, it will be as if the whole heaven
were bursting out in day. For this is what Christ calls the

single eye, and the whole body is inevitably full of light. How surely and how fast fly away the doubts, even as fogs are burned away by the sun.

Now to make this matter plain, I will suppose a case in which the dissolving of doubt in this manner is illustrated. Suppose that one of us, clear all the vices, having a naturally active-minded, inquiring habit, occupied largely with thoughts of religion,—never meaning to get away from the truth, but, as he thinks, to find it, only resolved to have a free mind, and not allow himself to be carried by force or fear of any thing but real conviction,—suppose that such a one going on thus, year by year, reading, questioning, hearing all the while the gospel in which he has been educated, sometimes impressed by it, but relapsing shortly into greater doubt than before, finds his religious beliefs wearing out, and vanishing, he knows not how, till finally he seems to really believe nothing. He has not meant to be an atheist, but he is astonished to find that he has nearly lost the conviction of God, and can not, if he would, say with any emphasis of conviction that God exists. The world looks blank, and he feels that existence is getting blank also to itself. This heavy charge of his possibly immortal being oppresses him, and he asks again and again, "What shall I do with it?" His hunger is complete, and his soul turns every way for bread. His friends do not satisfy him. His walks drag heavily. His suns do not rise, but only climb. A kind of leaden aspect overhangs the world. Till finally, pacing his chamber some day, there comes up suddenly the question,—"Is there, then, no truth that I do believe?—Yes, there is this one, now that I think of it, there is a distinction of right and wrong, that I never doubted, and I see not how I can; I am even quite sure of it." Then, forthwith, starts up the question, "Have I, then, ever taken the principle of right for my law? I have done right things as men speak, have I ever thrown my life out on the principle to become all it requires of me? No, I have not, consciously I have not. Ah! then here is something for me to do! No matter what becomes of my questions,—nothing ought to become of them, if I can not take a first principle so inevitably true and live in it." The very suggestion seems to be a kind of revelation; it is even a relief to feel the conviction it brings. "Here, then," he says, "will I begin. If there is a God, as I rather hope there is, and very dimly believe, he is a right God. If I have lost him in wrong, perhaps I shall find him in right. Will he not help me, or, perchance, even be discovered to me?" Now the decisive moment is come. He drops on his knees, and there he prays to the dim God dimly felt, confessing the dimness for honesty's sake, and asking for help, that he may begin a right life. He bows himself on it as he prays, choosing it to be henceforth his unalterable, eternal endeavor.

It is an awfully dark prayer, in the look of it, but the truest and best he can make,—the better and more true that he puts on orthodox colors on it; and the prayer and the vow are so profoundly meant that his soul is borne up into God's help, as it were by some unseen chariot, and permitted to see the opening of heaven even sooner than he opens his eyes. He rises and it is as if he had gotten wings. The whole sky is luminous about him,—it is the morning, as it were, of a new eternity. After this, all troublesome doubt of God's reality is gone, for he has found Him! A being so profoundly felt, must inevitably be.

Now this conversion, calling it by that name, as we properly should, may seem, in the apprehension of some, to be a conversion *for* the gospel and not *in* it or *by* it; a conversion

by the want of truth, more than by the power of truth. But
that will be a judgment more superficial than the facts per-
mit. No, it is exactly this: it is seeking first the kingdom of
God, and his righteousness,—exactly that and nothing less.
And the dimly groping cry for help—what is that but a feeling after God, if haply it may find him, and actually finding
him not far off. And what is the help obtained, but exactly
the true Christ-help? And the result—what also is that,
but the Kingdom of God within; righteousness, and peace,
and joy in the Holy Ghost?

[There is a story lodged in the little bedroom of one of
these dormitories, which, I pray God, his recording angel
may note, allowing it never to be lost.][2]

Now the result will be that a soul thus won to its integrity
of thought and meaning, will rapidly clear all tormenting
questions and difficulties. They are not all gone, but they
are going. Revelation, it may be, opens some troublesome
chapters. Preaching sometimes stumbles the neophyte,
when he might better be comforted by it. The great truths
of God often put him in a maze. The creation story, the
miracles, the incarnation, the trinity, the relations of justice
and mercy,—in all these he may only see, for a time, men
walking that have the look of trees. But the ship is launched,
he is gone to sea, and has the needle on board. He is going
now to sell every thing for the truth,—not the truth to keep
as a knowledge, but the truth to live by. He is going henceforth to be concentered in the right, nay, the righteousness
itself of God; and his prayers he will be hanging, O how
tenderly, on God, for the inward guidance of his Spirit. He

---

[2]The brackets indicate that Bushnell departed from his prepared manuscript and
related a personal experience.

will undertake shortly some point that is not cleared at once by the daylight of his new experience, and will, by and by, master it. That will give him courage to undertake shortly another, and he will go to it with new appetite. And so he will go on, not afraid to have questions even to the end of his life, and will be nowise disturbed by them. He will be in the gospel as an honest man, and will have it as a world of wonderfully grand, perpetually fresh discovery. He comes now to the lock with the key that opens it in his hand, fumbling no more in doubt, unresolved, because he has no key.

The menstruum, then, by which all doubts may be dissolved, appears to be sufficiently shown or provided. It only remains to add a few more promiscuous points of advice that relate to the general conduct of the mind in its new conditions.

1. Be never afraid of doubt. Perhaps a perfectly upright angelic mind well enough might, though I am not sure even of that. We, at least, are in the fog eternal of wrong, and there is no way for us to get clear but to prove all things and hold fast. Make free use of all the intelligence God has given you, only taking care to use it in a consciously supreme allegiance to right and to God. Your questions then will only be your helpers, and the faster they come, the better will be your progress in the truth.

2. Be afraid of all sophistries, and tricks, and strifes of disingenuous argument. Doting about questions, and doubting about them are very different things. Any kind of cunning art or dodge of strategem in your words and arguments will do you incalculable mischief. They will damage the sense of truth, which is the worst possible kind of damage. False arguments make the soul itself false, and

then a false, uncandid soul can see nothing as it is. No man can fitly seek after truth who does not hold truth in the deepest reverence. Truth must be sacred even as God, else it is nothing.

3. Have it as a fixed principle also, that getting into any scornful way is fatal. Scorn is dark, and has no eyes; for the eyes it thinks it has are only sockets in the place of eyes. Doubt is reason, scorn is disease. One simply questions, searching after evidence; the other has got above evidence, and turns to mockery the modest way that seeks it. Even if truth were found, it could not stay in any scorning man's bosom. The tearing voice, the scowling brow, the leer, the sneer, the jeer, would make the place a robber's cave to it, and drive the delicate and tender guest to make his escape at the first opportunity. There was never a scorner that gave good welcome to truth. Knaves can as well harbor honesty, and harlots chastity, as scorners truth.

4. Never settle upon any thing as true, because it is safer to hold it than not. I will not say that any one is to have it as a point of duty to be damned, or willing to be, for the truth. I only say that truth brings often great liabilities of cost, and we must choose it, cost what it will. To accept the Bible even because it is safest, as some persons do, and some ministers very lightly preach, is to do the greatest dishonor both to it and to the soul. Such faith is cowardly, and is even a lie besides. It is basing a religion, not in truth, but in the doctrine of chances, and reducing the salvation of God to a bill of insurance. If the Bible is true, believe it, but do not mock it by assuming for a creed the mere chance that it may be. For the same reason, take religion, not because it will be good for your family, or good for the state, but because it is the homage due inherently from man to

God and the kingdom of God. What more flashy conceit can there be, than a religion accepted as a domestic or political nostrum?

5. Have it as a law never to put force on the mind, or try to make it believe; because it spoils the mind's integrity, and when that is gone, what power of advance in the truth is left? I know very well that the mind's integrity is far enough gone already, and that all our doubts and perpetual self-defeats come upon us for just that reason. All the more necessary is it that we come into what integrity we can, and stay there. Let the soul be immovable as rock, by any threat of danger, any feeling of risk, any mere scruple, any call to believe by sheer, self-compelling will. The soul that is anchored in right will do no such thing. There must, of course, be no obstinacy, no stiff holding out after conviction has come. There must be tenderness, docility, and, with these, a most firmly kept equilibrium. There must be no gustiness of pride or self-will to fog the mind and keep right conviction away.

6. Never be in a hurry to believe, never try to conquer doubts against time. Time is one of the grand elements in thought as truly as in motion. If you can not open a doubt to-day, keep it till to-morrow; do not be afraid to keep it for whole years. One of the greatest talents in religious discovery, is the finding how to hang up questions and let them hang without being at all anxious about them. Turn a free glance on them now and then as they hang, move freely about them, and see them, first on one side, and then on another, and by and by when you turn some corner of thought, you will be delighted and astonished to see how quietly and easily they open their secret and let you in!

What seemed perfectly insoluble will clear itself in a wondrous revelation. It will not hurt you, nor hurt the truth, if you should have some few questions left to be carried on with you when you go hence, for in that more luminous state, most likely, they will soon be cleared,—only a thousand others will be springing up even there, and you will go on dissolving still your new sets of questions, and growing mightier and more deep-seeing for eternal ages.

Now, my friends, it would not be strange if I had in the audience before me all sorts of doubts, and varieties of questions, all grades of incipient unbelief, or, it may be, of unbelief not incipient, but ripe and in full seed. But I have one and the same work for you all, that is, look after the day, and the night itself will join you in it. Or, better still, set your clock by the sun; then it will be right all day, and even all night besides, and be ready when he rises, pointing its finger to the exact minute where he stands, in the circle of his swift motion. Be right, that is, first of all, in what you know, and your soul will be faithfully chiming with all you ought to know. All evidences are with you then, and you with them. Even if they seem to be hid, they will shortly appear, and bring you their light. But this being right implies a great deal, observe, and especially these two things: —First, that you pray for all the help you can get; for without this you can not believe, or feel, that you truly want to be right. Secondly, that you consent, in advance, to be a christian, and begin a religious life, fulfilling all the sacrifices of such a life, provided you may find it necessary to do so, in order to carry out and justify yourself in acting up to the principle you have accepted. Undertaking to be right, only resolving not to be a christian, is but a mockery of right. You must go where it carries you. You must even be a

Mahometan, a Jew, a Pagan,—any thing to have a clear conscience. There is no likelihood, it is true, that you will have to be either of these, but there is an almost certainty that you must be a christian. Be that as it may, you must consent to go where right conviction carries you. And there is even some proper doubt whether you can get out of this place of worship without being carried to Christ, if you undertake to go out as a thoroughly right man. For Christ is but the Sun of Righteousness, and you will assuredly find that, in being joined to the RIGHT, you are joined eternally to him, and walking with him in the blessed daylight of his truth.

II

Phillips Brooks:
Preacher and Pastor

Phillips Brooks is commonly recognized as a great preacher, one of the greatest America has produced. It is not so commonly recognized that he was also a great pastor. In the introductory chapter we quoted Phillips Brooks to the effect that the work of the preacher and pastor ought never to be separated, for they are "not two tasks but one." His own ministry is an excellent example of the principle he emphasized.

The attitudes and the faithfulness with which he served as a pastor are well worth the study of anyone interested in the field of pastoral care, and the relationship of his preaching and his pastoral work is well worth the study of anyone interested in life-situation preaching.

Although he was amazingly successful from the pulpit, and in spite of the fact that he delighted in the solitude of his study, Brooks chose to spend much time with his people. He found his inspiration from contact with life. He was extraordinarily sensitive to human need. He spent his afternoons calling upon his people, especially the poor, the sick, and the troubled. He once said that he wished he could do nothing but make pastoral calls. Wherever there was need, he would go. When people were in trouble, he would go and sit with them for hours, just listening to them talk.

He was particularly concerned for the sick. A. V. G. Allen, his friend and biographer, said that wherever he went his personality carried power, courage, and hopefulness. "A mysterious influence seemed to go forth from him for good, for strength and life, even when he sat down in silence by the bedside and no need was felt for words."[1] On one occasion he was leaving for a reception when word came from the hospital that a colored man had sent for him. Brooks went at once and did not arrive at the reception until 11 o'clock. A physician expressed surprise that he had not sent an assistant, but Brooks said that the man had sent for him.

• Brooks not only went to the people; the people also came to Brooks. They came in great numbers, from near and far; not only members of Trinity Church, but people of every creed and every nationality; not only residents of Boston, but people from all over the state and country. It was said that his parish knew no limits. His house was a refuge for all who were in trouble. Allen said that his personality "attracted as by a magnet those who were in trouble." He was constantly confronted with some problem of suffering or sorrow. Persons came at any hour of the day or night, but he refused to seclude himself or to set limited hours when they might come. When it was suggested that he do this, he replied that it might not be convenient for the individuals who wanted counsel. It was one of the rules of his ministry that the man who wanted to see him was the man he wanted to see. Leighton Parks, who lived with him for several weeks, was amazed at the frequency with which the doorbell rang, so he kept a record for his own information. He discovered that the bell rang on an average of

---

[1] Allen, op. cit., Vol. II, p. 807.

once every five minutes in the entire day. There was someone in the study almost continuously, while others were
waiting in the reception room or in the dining room. Yet
the person in the study was made to feel that, at the moment, this was the one thing that Phillips Brooks had
to do and that he was interested only in this person's problem. And, at that moment, this was true.

People brought him every type of problem. In critical
moments of their lives they thought of Phillips Brooks.
They came with personal problems, family problems, and
religious problems, seeking counsel, comfort, and advice.
He preached regularly at Appleton Chapel at Harvard and,
after each service, he was almost besieged by students for
interviews. He was the confidant of countless clergymen,
especially young men who sought his advice. His correspondence with those who sought his help was tremendous.

All of this was in the background of his preaching. He
once said that if he could not see people individually he
could not preach. His sermons dealt with life. He spoke
very rapidly and rather informally. Lord Bryce said of
him, "He speaks to his audience as a man might speak to
a friend." A visitor at Trinity Church used to say that the
thing that impressed him about Phillips Brooks's preaching
was his obvious love for his congregation.

He was so much concerned about people that he made a
careful, almost scientific, study of consolation. We have
chosen for inclusion here a sermon on "The Purpose and
Use of Comfort."

THE PURPOSE AND USE OF COMFORT

By Phillips Brooks

*Blessed be the God of all comfort, who com-
forteth us in all our tribulation, that we may be
able to comfort them which are in any trouble,
by the comfort wherewith we ourselves are comforted of God.*

—2 Cor. 1:3, 4.

The desire for comfort may be a very high or a very low,
a noble or a most ignoble wish. It is like the love of life,
the wish to keep on living, which may be full of courage and
patience, or may be nothing but a cowardly fear of death.
We know what kind of comfort it must have been that St.
Paul prayed for, and for which he was thankful when it
came. We have all probably desired comfort which he
would have scorned, and prayed to God in tones which he
would have counted unworthy alike of God and of himself.

And the difference in the way in which people ask comfort of God, no doubt, depends very largely upon the reason
why they ask it, upon what it is that makes them wish that
God would take away their pain and comfort them. The
nobleness of actions, we all know, depends more upon the
reasons why we do them than on the acts themselves. Very
few acts are so essentially noble that they may not be done
for an ignoble reason, and so become ignoble. Very few
acts are so absolutely mean that some light may not be cast
through them by a bright motive burning within. And so
it is not merely with what we do, but with what happens

to us. It is not our fortune in life, our sorrow, or our joy; it is the explanation which we give of it to ourselves, the depth to which we see down into it, that makes our lives significant or insignificant to us.

All this, I think, applies to what St. Paul says about the comfort which God had given him. He gave to it its deepest and most unselfish reason, and so the fact of God's comforting him became the exaltation and the strengthening of his life. I should like to study his feeling about it all with you this morning. Out of your closets and pews, from many hearts that need it, hearts sore and wounded with the world, there go up prayers for comfort. This verse of St. Paul seems to me to shine with a supreme motive for such prayers as those, a motive which perhaps as we first look at it will seem overstrained and impossible; but which I hope we shall see is really capable of being felt, and of stirring to their deepest depths the desire and the gratitude of a strong man.

It does not matter what the special trouble was for which God had comforted St. Paul. It happened to be a certain deep anxiety about his church at Corinth. But it might have been anything. The point is this—that Paul thanked God because the comfort which had come to him gave him the power to comfort other people. "Blessed be the God of all comfort, who comforteth us in all our tribulations, that we may be able to comfort them which are in any trouble." Now, my dear friends, try to recall the joy and peace and thankfulness that have ever filled your hearts when you became thoroughly sure that God had relieved you from some great danger, or opened His hand and shed upon you some great blessing. Think how you thanked Him. Remember how the sense that He loved you occupied your soul. Think how your sense of privilege exalted you and solemnized you. Think how your own happiness filled you with kindliness to other people. But ask yourself at the same time, "Did any such thought as this come up first and foremost to my mind, and seem to me the most precious part of all my blessing, that God had done this for me just to make me a fitter and more transparent medium through which He might send his comfort to other men? When He lifted me up from the gates of death did I thank Him most of all that my experience of danger and deliverance had made clear to some poor sufferer beside me how truly our God is the Lord of life and death? When He came and filled with His own presence the awful blank of my bereavement, did I praise Him most devoutly that my refilled and recreated life could become a gospel to other men of the satisfaction of His perfect friendship?" But this was the beauty of God's comfort to St. Paul. "Blessed be God who comforteth us, that we may be able to comfort them which are in any trouble."

In the first place, then, I think the power of Paul or of any man to grasp and realize this high idea of the purpose of the help which God sends, shows a very clear understanding that it is really God who sends the help. Indeed, I think no man can really mount up to the idea that God truly and personally cares for him enough to reach down and turn the bitterness of his cup to sweetness, without being, as it were, compelled to look beyond himself. All strong emotions, all really great ideas, outgo our individual life, and make us feel our human nature. If you are not sure that any mercy comes to you from God; if, whatever pious words you use about it, the recovery of your health, or the saving of your fortune, seems to you a piece of luck, some good thing which has dropped down upon you from the clouds, then you may be meanly and miserably selfish about it. You shut it up within the jealous walls of your own life. It is a light which you have struck out for yourself, and may burn in your own lantern. But if the light came down from God, if He gave you this blessing, it is too big for you to keep to yourself. He must have meant it for a wider circle than your little life can cover, and it breaks through your selfishness to find for itself the mission that it claims. Oh, if men who are disgusted at their own selfishness and unsympathetic narrowness, and who try to break through it and come to their fellow-men in love, but cannot, would learn this higher and profounder method, that the only way really to come close to and to care for men is to realize God; the only way to love the children is to know the Father; the only way to make it our joy and mission to help mankind is to feel all through us the certainty that the help which has come to us has come from God!

Go on a little farther. A man whose first thought about any mercy to himself is that God means by it to help other people, must have something else besides this strong belief that his mercy does really come from God. He must have a genuine unselfishness and a true humility. He must have a habit of looking out beyond himself, a yearning and instinctive wish to know how what comes to him will change the lot and life of other people; and, along with this, a lowly estimate of his own self, a true humbleness of self-esteem. Put these together into a nature and you clear away those obstructions which, in so many men, stop God's mercies short, and absorb, as personal privileges, what they were meant to radiate as blessings to mankind. Think of it even in reference to the lowest things. Who is the man whom we rejoice to see possessing wealth? Who is the man whose making money on the street delights us, because it means benefaction and help to other men? It is the reverent, the unselfish, and the humble man. It is the man who, as the treasure pours in at his doors, stands saying over it, "God sent this;" and, "I am not worthy of this; He could not have sent it just for me;" and, "Where are my brethren?" Reverence, Humility, Unselfishness. Those are the elements of true stewardship even in the lowest things, and also in the highest. Who is the man who, in his bereavement or his pain, receiving comfort from God radiates it, so that the world is richer by the help the Lord has given him? It is the reverent, the unselfish, and the humble man. The sunlight falls upon a clod, and the clod drinks it in, is warmed by it itself, but lies as black as ever, and sheds out no light. But the sun touches a diamond, and the diamond almost chills itself as it sends out in radiance on every side the light that has fallen on it. So God helps one man bear his pain, and nobody but that one man is a whit the richer. God comes to another sufferer, reverent, unselfish, humble, and the lame leap, and the dumb speak, and the wretched are comforted all around by the radiated comfort of that happy soul. Our lot has been dark indeed if we have not known some souls, reverent, unselfish, humble, who not merely caught and drank in themselves, but poured out on other sufferers, on us, the comfort of God.

I know one danger which I may seem to incur as I speak thus. It may appear as if in order to find a deep, far-reaching purpose in God's goodness to our souls, to trace it out into designs for other people, we had to take away something from its freedom and spontaneousness; as if it interfered with that first consciousness of the religious life, the first and most surprising, as it is also the last and sweetest and most inexhaustible, that God loves each of us dis-

tinctly, separately, and blesses each of us out of His personal love. Nothing must interfere with that. Whatever
mercy falls into our lot must be felt warm with the personal
love of Him who sends it. It would be better to lose all the
larger and longer thoughts of God's care for the world, and
think of Him, as men have thought, merely in the light of
His love for the individual, than to become so absorbed in
the larger thought that the individual should seem to be only
the unconsidered machinery through which His power
reached the world, blessed by accident, as it were, and on
the way, as the blessing sped to some more general and dis-
tant need. But we are reduced to no such dilemma. The
simpler ideas of religion include the more profound, and
open into them without losing their own simplicity. The
soul, I think, which has really reached the idea that what
God does for it has purposes beyond it in the good of others,
comes to a deeper knowledge of the love of God for it. It
finds itself honored with confidence and use, as well as
gratified with happiness. The older children of a family
gradually come to the knowledge of what deeper purposes
run through the government of the household. When a
child is young, it seems as if his father's purpose concerning
him were just that he should find every hour pleasant, and
be happy all the time. As he grows up he learns that his
father is treating him with reference to something which
lies deeper than his happiness, and also that what his father
does to him has reference to the whole family, and is part
of a larger scheme. Does that lessen the warmth of his
personal gratitude and love? Not unless he is a very mean-
minded and jealous child indeed. If he has any largeness
of character, it all comes out. A new sacredness appears
in the kindness when its designs are known, and as gratitude

grows reasonable it grows deeper. So it is with gratitude to God. The superstitious devotee begs for a kindness which is to have no end beyond himself. He asks for comfort and help as if he had to tease it from a God of whims; but the Christian asks, as his highest privilege, to be taken into the purposes of a purposeful Father, and counts it the best part of the stream which refreshes his life, that it goes on through his to refresh some other life beyond. Oh, let us never fear that in making God considerate and reasonable we shall lose His affection; let us never try to keep His love by denying His law. Let us be sure that the more we realize His vaster purposes, the more dearly we can feel His personal care.

And one thing more let me say here. This higher thought of God and His blessings will always be easier and more real to us in proportion as we dwell habitually upon the profounder and more spiritual of His mercies. If what I am in the habit of thanking God for is mainly food and clothes and house, it will not be easy for me to realize the deepest purposes for which God gives me those things; it will be very easy for me to take them as if the final purpose of them was that I might be warm and well-fed. But if what I thank Him for is spiritual strength, the way in which He helps me bear pain, resist temptation, and feed upon spiritual joy,—in one word, if what I thank Him for most is not that He gives me His gifts, but that He gives me Himself,— then I cannot resist the tendency of that mercy to outgrow my life. The more spiritual is a man's religion, the more expansive and broad it always is. A stream may leave its deposits in the pool it flows through, but the stream itself hurries on to other pools in the thick woods; and so God's gifts a soul may selfishly appropriate, but God Himself, the more truly a soul possess Him, the more truly it will long and try to share Him.

Thus I have tried to picture the man who in the profoundest way accepts and values God's mercies. You see how clear his superiority is. The Pharisee says, "I thank Thee that I am not as other men are," and evidently it is his difference from other men that he values most, and he means to keep himself different from other men as long as possible. The Christian says, "I thank Thee that Thou hast made me this, because it is a sign and may be made a means of bringing other men to the same help and joy." You see how different the two men are: one is hard and selfish; the other is warm and generous. And yet there must be people here this morning who have knelt side by side and both said sincerely, "We bless Thee for our creation, preservation, and all the blessings of this life," who were as far apart from one another as the Pharisee is from the Christian spirit.

But having said thus much in general about the way in which men receive God's comforts, now I should like to take, one after another, a few of the special helps which God gives to men, and see, very briefly, how what I have been saying applies to each of them.

1. The first of the comforts of God to which I would apply our truth is the comfort which God sends a man when he is in religious doubt. And that does not by any means always take the shape of a solution of his difficulties, and a filling of every darkness with perfect light. God may do that. God does often do that for men. I think that none of us ever ought to believe that any religious difficulty of his is hopeless, and to give it up in despair. We ought always to stand looking at every such difficulty, owning its darkness,

but ready to see it brighten as the east brightens with the rising of the sun.   Many of our religious doubts are like buildings which stand beside the road which we are travelling, which, as we first come in sight of them, we cannot understand.   They are all in confusion.   They show no plan. We have come on them from the rear, from the wrong side. But, as we travel on, the road sweeps round them.   We come in front of them.   Their design unsnarls itself, and we understand the beauty of wall and tower and window.   So we come to many religious questions from the rear, from the wrong side.   Let us keep on along the open road of righteousness.   Some day we shall perhaps face them and see their orderly beauty.

No doubt God does thus answer our questions for us sometimes if we will "walk in His ways."   But he knows little of the abundance of God's mercy who thinks that there is no other comfort for the doubting man than this. He has had little experience of God who has not often felt how sometimes, with a question still unanswered, a deep doubt in the soul unsolved, the Father will fold about His doubting child a sense of Himself so deep, so true, so self-witnessing, that the child is content to carry his unanswered question because of the unanswerable assurance of his Father which he has received.   Is that a fancy?   Surely not.   Surely you are comforting your child just in that way every day; comforting him with your love, and the peace of your presence, which passeth all his understanding, for the hundred questions which you cannot answer, and the hundred puzzles which you cannot make him understand.   Suppose God gives that sort of comfort to any man.   Thenceforth the doubter goes with his curious doubts, not solved, but wrapt about and lost in the richness of a personal faith.

But tell me, is it the gain of that one doubter only? Is the world no richer? Is no other questioner helped? Oh, when I see how few men are aided by the arguments with which their friends plead for their faith, compared with those to whom religion becomes a clear reality from the sight of some fellow-man who is evidently living with God, who carries the life of God wherever he goes; when I see how the real difficulty of multitudes of bewildered men is not this or that unsolved problem, but the whole incapacity of comprehending God; when I see this, I understand how the best boon that God can give to any group of men must often be to take one of them—the greatest of them it may be, the least of them it may be—and, bearing witness of Himself to him, set him to bearing that witness of the Lord to his brethren which only a man surrounded and filled with God can bear.

And when we look at the other side, at the doubter himself, and his feeling about the removal of his doubt, it is even more plain. I can find no certainty about religious things, and I hardly dare ask for certainty. It seems like haggling and arguing with God to tell him of my doubts. Who am I that He should care to convince me and answer my questions? It is a bad mood, but it is common enough. But if I can count my enlightenment as something greater than my own release from doubt; if I can see it as part of the process by which "the light that lighteneth every man" is a lowly spreading through the world, then it no longer is insignificant. I dare to hope for it. I dare to pray for it. I make myself ready for it. I cast aside frivolity and despair, the two benighteners of the human soul, and when God comes and over, under, nay, through every doubt proves Himself to me, I take Him with a certainty which is as humble as it is solemn and sure.

2. Turn to another of the consolations which God sends to men; the way He proves to us that the soul is more than the body. In the breakage or decay of physical power He brings out spiritual richness and strength. This was something that St. Paul knew well. Only two chapters later in this same epistle there comes the great verse where he describes it. "Though our outward man perish, yet the inward man is renewed day by day." It is something whose experience is repeated constantly on every side of us. It is hard for us to imagine how flat and shallow human life would be if there were taken out of it this constant element, the coming up of the spiritual where the physical has failed; and so, as the result of this, the impression, made even upon men who seem to trust most in the physical, that there is a spiritual life which lies deeper, on which their profoundest reliance must and may be placed. A man who has been in the full whirl of prosperous business fails in these hard-pressed days, and then for the first time he learns the joy of conscious integrity preserved through all temptations, and of daily trust in God for daily bread. A man who never knew an ache or pain comes to a break in health, from which he can look out into nothing but years of sickness; and then the soul within him, which has been so borne along in the torrent of bodily health that it has seemed almost like a mere part and consequence of the bodily condition, separates itself, claims its independence and supremacy, and stands strong in the midst of weakness, calm in the very centre of the turmoil and panic of the aching body. The temper of the fickle people changes, and the favorite of yesterday becomes the victim of to-day; but in his martyrdom for the first time he sees the full value of the truth he dies for, and thanks the flames that have lighted up its

preciousness. Now ask yourself in all these cases if it must not be an element in the comfort which fills the sick room, or gathers about the martyr's stake, that by this revelation of the spiritual through the broken physical life other men may learn its value. This is what makes the sick rooms and the martyr fires reasonable. In them has been made manifest by suffering that the soul is really more than the body, that the soul can triumph when the body has nothing left but disease and misery. There are young people here looking forward to their lives, wondering what God has in reserve for them in these mysterious and beautiful years which lie before them. It may be health, strength, joy, activity. I trust it is. But you must own that it would be no sign of God's displeasure, but rather of His truest love, if the life which He assigned should prove to be all comprised in this: that by some form of suffering and disappointment you were first to find out for yourself, and then to manifest to some circle of your fellow-men, that the soul is more precious than the body, and has a happiness and strength which no bodily experience can touch. What would you not suffer if your life could be made a beacon to show the world that?

This is the secret of great men. And in all the greatest men there is some sense of this always present. No man has come to true greatness who has not felt in some degree that his life belongs to his race, and that what God gives him He gives him for mankind. The different degrees of this consciousness are really what makes the different degrees of greatness in men. If you take your man full of acuteness, at the top of his specialty, of vast knowledge, of exhaustless skill, and ask yourself where the mysterious lack is which keeps you from thinking that man great,—why it is that although he may be a great naturalist, or a great merchant, or a great inventor, he is not a great man,—the answer will be here, that he is selfish: that what God gives him stops in himself; that he has no such essential humanity as to make his life a reservoir from which refreshment is distributed, or a point of radiation for God's light. And then if you take another man, rude, simple, untaught, in whom it is hard to find special attainments or striking points of character, but whom you instinctively call great, and ask yourself the reason of that instinct, I think you find it in the fact that that man has this quality: that his life does take all which it receives, not for its own use but in trust; that in the highest sense it is unselfish, so that by it God reaches men, and it is His greatness that you feel in it. For greatness after all, in spite of its name, appears to be not so much a certain size as a certain quality in human lives. It may be present in lives whose range is very small. There is greatness in a mother's life whose utter unselfishness fills her household with the life and love of God, transmitted through her consecration. There is greatness in a child's life who is patient under a wrong and shows the world at some new point the dignity of self-restraint and the beauty of conquered passions. And thence we rise until we come to Christ and find the perfection of His human greatness in His transmissiveness; in the fact that what He was as man, He was not for Himself alone but for all men, for mankind. All through the range of human life, from lowest up to highest, any religious conception of human greatness must be ultimately reducible to this: a quality in any man by which he is capable first of taking into himself, and then of distributing through himself to others, some part of the life of God.

I spoke just now of Jesus and His greatness. It seems to me that most of the struggles of theology to define His work are really trying to get hold of and utter this idea: that in Him was the perfect power of uttering God to men and of being full of God not for Himself only but for mankind. His headship of our race, His mediatorship, His atonement, are various ways of stating this idea. Everything that He was and did, He was and did for us. He lived his life, He died his death, for us. He took sorrow for us. He took joy and comfort for us also. Let me not say that Christ saves us only by what He suffered for us. He saves us by what He enjoyed for us too. The completeness and unity of His salvation lies in the completeness and unity with which His whole life, in its joy and pain together, lies between us and God, so that through it God comes to us and we go to God. Let us always pray that we may lose the blessing of no part of the complete mediatorship of our Mediator.

3. There is one other of the comforts of God to which I hoped that we might apply our truth, but I must take only a moment for it. I mean the comfort which God gives a man who has found out his sin and has repented of it. That comfort is forgiveness,—forgiveness promised by Christ, assured by the whole loving nature of God, and sealed by the new life of thankful obedience which begins at once in the forgiven man. And what shall we say of that forgiveness? Is it only for the forgiven man that it is bestowed, that God loves to bestow it so? It often seems to me as if we took too low a ground in pleading with the man living in sin and indifference to turn around, to be converted and live another life. We tell him of his danger. That puts it on the lowest ground. We assure him that no man can go on in wilful

sin in a universe over which a good God reigns, without
sooner or later coming to unhappiness, nay, without really
being in unhappiness all the time, however it may seem to
him. We go higher than that: we tell him of the happiness
of the life with God. We assure him of faculties in himself,
capable of a kind of pleasure which he does not know, which
will come out to their true enjoyment if he will only come
to God. We tell him of the heaven of the inner life here,
and then point onward to the dim but certain joys of the
heaven that stands with its golden walls and gates of pearl
in the splendor of the revelation there. Many men hear and
believe. Many men hear and do not believe. Suppose we
took a higher strain; suppose we cast all selfishness aside;
suppose we pointed to a world all full of wickedness, a
world self-willed, rebellious against God; suppose we went
to men and said: "Think of this. Every time any man
humbly takes God's forgiveness, enters into Christ's service,
begins a godly life, that man becomes a new witness to this
world of how strong and good the Saviour is. Here is
Christ. There are the men who need Him. If you will let
Him fill and possess your life, He will make these men see
Him through you. And look, how they need to see Him!
Not for yourself now, but for them, for Him, take His forgiveness and give up yourself inwardly and outwardly to
Him." So used one grows to find men respond to the
noblest motives who are deaf to a motive which is less noble,
that I am ready to believe that there are men among you,
whose faces I know, whom I have so often urged to be Christians, who might feel this higher appeal. Is it nothing that
by a new purity and devotion in your life, brought there
by obedience to Christ, you may help men out of their sins
to Him? His promises seem to the men you meet too good
to be true, so glorious and sweet that they are unreal. Take

them to yourself. Let them shine in their manifest power through the familiar windows of your life. Be a new man in Christ for these men's sake Put your hand in His, that as He leads you other men, who have turned away from Him, may look and see you walking with Him, learn to love Him through your love. I do not believe any man ever yet genuinely, humbly, thoroughly gave himself to Christ without some other finding Christ through him. I wish it might tempt some of your souls to the higher life. I hope it may. At least I am sure that it may add a new sweetness and nobleness to the consecration which some young heart is making of itself today, if it can hear, down the new path on which it is entering, not merely the great triumphant chant of personal salvation, "Unto Him that loved us and washed us from our sins be glory and dominion;" but also the calmer, deeper thanksgiving of usefulness, "Blessed be the God of comfort, who comforteth us that we may be able to comfort them that are in tribulation."

Such are a few of the illustrations and applications of the truth which I have tried to define and to urge upon you this morning. The truth is that we are our best when we try to be it not for ourselves alone, but for our brethren; and that we take God's gifts most completely for ourselves when we realize that He sends them to us for the benefit of other men, who stand beyond us needing them. I have spoken very feebly, unless you have felt something of the difference which it would make to all of us if this truth really took possession of us. It would make our struggles after a higher life so much more intense as they become more noble. "For their sakes I sanctify myself," said Jesus; and He hardly ever said words more wonderful than those. There was the power by which He was holy; the world was to be made holy, was to be sanctified through Him. I am sure that you or I could indeed be strengthened to meet some great experience of pain if we really believed that by our suffering we were to be made luminous with help to other men. They are to get from us painlessly what we have got most painfully from God. There is the power of the bravest martyrdom and the hardest work that the world has ever seen.

And again, it would make our spiritual lives and experiences more recognizable and certain things. Not by mere moods, not by how I feel to-day or how I felt yesterday, may I know whether I am indeed living the life of God, but only by knowing that God is using me to help others. No mood is so bright that it can do without that warrant. No mood is so dark that, if it has that, it need despair. It is good for us to think no grace or blessing truly ours till we are aware that God has blessed some-one else with it through us.

I have not painted an ideal and impossible picture to you to-day, my friends. This truth and all the motives that flow from it may really fill your life. They filled the life of Christ. Come near to Him; be like Him, and they shall fill yours. So your Gethsemane and the angels that come to you after it may be precious to you as His were to Him, not only for the peace which they brought Him, but because they were to be the fountain of strength and hope to countless souls forever. May God grant us something of the privilege of Christ, which was to live a manly life for God's sake, and also to live a godly life for men's sake: for it was thus that He was a mediator between God and man.

III

Charles Jefferson:
The Minister as Shepherd

Charles Jefferson served for many years as the pastor of
Broadway Tabernacle in New York City. Newspaper men
called it the "skyscraper church." Although he ministered
to a city congregation in the heart of a great metropolis,
when he thought of the pastor he thought in terms of a shepherd. His little book which he called *The Minister as Shepherd* is recognized as one of the classics of pastoral theology.
A few sentences from this book will give something of the
spirit in which he considered the work of the pastor.

There is always some one ailing in the parish,
not physically only, but mentally, morally, spiritually. . . . Here is a field in which the minister is
called upon to put forth his skill and strength. His
mission is to the sick, and all sick people are not
sick with the same sickness, nor do they all require
the same remedies or the same kind of nursing.
Nowhere else does the minister need such piercing
insight, such fine powers of discrimination, such
skill in diagnosis, and such ability to cope with
subtle and mysterious forces, as here. There are
ministers who hardly enter into this great realm
of pastoral service. Sick consciences are in their

parish, but they do not know how to treat them. Wounded hearts are bleeding, but they do not know how to staunch the flow of blood. Rereaved and other grief-stricken souls are mourning, but they do not know how to speak the healing word. Spirits are sick unto death, but they can bring them no relief. There are those who are possessed of demons, and the pastor does not know how to cast them out. The whole science of spiritual therapeutics is unknown to him, and followers of Jesus in many cases suffer on for years with diseases from which an expert spiritual physician could have delivered them. There are in many a parish cases of arrested religious development, instances of moral paralysis, sad attacks of spiritual prostration which could be relieved and cured if only the minister understood better the nature of the soul and the remedies offered to human minds in Jesus Christ.[1]

It was from this book that we quoted in the Introduction when we referred to Jefferson's saying that the pastor does not cease to be a pastor when he enters the pulpit but then assumes one of his most exacting pastoral tasks. For him the tasks of preaching and pastoral work were two parts of one common purpose.

It was his custom to preach a sermon on nature once a year. He was preaching to a city congregation and he felt that "city congregations are in special need of the healing influences of the woods and fields." These sermons might be considered the preventive type of preaching. They are

---

[1]From *The Minister as Shepherd,* by Charles Jefferson, copyright 1912, Thomas Y. Crowell Company. Used by permission.

not designed to solve a particular problem, but to make people aware of resources that enrich and strengthen life. He felt that city life presented certain difficulties by its very nature. "A city," he said, "shuts men in behind walls of marble and steel, brick and granite, and these are not a wholesome environment for human nerves." When he speaks of the "city man," he sounds very contemporary. "In the street he is jostled and hustled by the crowd. In his business he contends with the perversities of many types of human nature. . . . City life is always tending to become feverish and abnormal."

To counteract these influences he preached his sermons on nature. "Now and again, one needs to escape from the gloomy canyons of city streets," he said, ". . . and look upon the world which God has made." He saw nature as the "great rest-giver," a "great physician." "In the city we become excitable and hot. We move at a headlong pace. The interruptions and collisions are many. We need a physician who can take the fever from the brow and the fret out of the heart. Nature has remedies for all who are sick. . . . She is sensible and strong. . . . She keeps, for ever, an even pulse. We need her. To think of her quiets the heart; to gaze on her calm face is refreshment and power."

Some of the titles are quite unique. He preached sermons on clouds and sunsets, storms and lakes. The sermon we have included here is on "Shadows," although any of these others might have been selected. "Nature," he said, "is a giver of joy. The Kingdom of God is a Kingdom of Joy, but joyousness is not one of the notes of the life of the average Christian. We are not joyous because we have not advanced far into the Kingdom of God. As the years increase, many of the fountains of happiness begin to fail. He is a

wise man who keeps as many fountains as possible flowing.
The love of Nature is an unfailing fountain of joy."[2]   To
keep alive these fountains of joy he preached these sermons.
Undoubtedly many people in his congregation left the
Broadway Tabernacle aware of a new resource for the en-
richment of life which they had not noticed or used before.

---

[2]From *Nature Sermons,* copyright 1935 by Fleming H. Revell Company. Used by
permission.

SHADOWS[1]

By Charles Jefferson

In this sermon I want to think with you about shadows. I like to take something that is familiar and common, something which you have at your door and which it is not necessary for you to travel half-way round the world to find.

Shadows are the most ethereal and insubstantial of all the phenomena we have thus far studied. There is nothing so light and so thin and so bodiless as a shadow. You cannot pick one up with the fingers of your hand. If you pick it up at all, it must be with the fingers of your mind. A shadow weighs nothing. You throw it on the scales, but you cannot weigh it—it has no weight. I have often wondered what a kitten thinks when, for the first time, it pounces down upon a shadow thinking that it is going to catch something, and suddenly discovers that there is something in this world into which a kitten cannot get its claws!

And so a shadow has become a metaphor, and has a fixed place in our English speech. We have many words expressive of that which is infinitesimally small, but when we push language to the limit, we use the word "shadow." A mother says to her little boy: "You had not a shadow of an excuse for doing that." She might have said: "You had not an atom of an excuse, or a splinter, or an iota, or a scintilla, or a trace of an excuse." But if the mother wishes to say the strongest thing that it is possible to say, she uses the word "shadow." When we have not the shadow of an excuse we

[1]From *Nature Sermons*, copyright 1935 by Fleming R. Revell Company. Used by permission.

have no excuse at all. When you push human thought to the vanishing point, then you fall back on the word "shadow."

Not only is a shadow ethereal and insubstantial, but it is also evanescent. It is constantly changing. It lives for a little time and then passes away. You look at it and turn your head away, in a moment you look at it again, and it is changed; it is longer or shorter, it is thicker or more slender. A shadow cannot possibly remain an hour the same. A shadow is as changeable and as fidgety as a little child. You look at a shadow and go away for a season, and when you come back it is gone. That shadow will not come back again. It has gone for ever. A shadow is not only empty but it is also fleeting. Shakespeare understood the weight and worth of English words as probably no other man has ever understood them. When he uses a word for the expression of a certain thought we may be sure that it is the best word that can be chosen. There is a fine and faultless fidelity in his choice of words. When it dawns upon Macbeth that life is empty and also transitory, what is the first word which Shakespeare puts into his mouth? "Life's but a walking shadow." That tells the whole sad story. Shakespeare goes on according to his fashion piling word on word in order to deepen the impression, but when he comes to the end of the sentence he can say only this: "signifying nothing." All had been told in the word with which he started.

Now shadows are the children of God. They are His creation, they are foreordained by Him. You cannot conceive of a universe like this without shadows in it. There cannot be a universe with the sun and moon and stars, and the planet revolving on its axis, and moving beings on the surface of the planet, without shadows. The Eternal planned a universe with shadows in it. He said: "Let there be shadows," and shadows there were. When He looked upon the completed universe the writer of the first book of the Bible says: "God saw that it was good." This means that He saw that the shadows were good, they enhanced the beauty of it all. And all these shadows are obedient to God's eternal law. There has never been a disobedient shadow since the world began. All of them have been obedient to the God who created them.

I love to look through books which I have no time to read. Life is too short to read many books, but there are many books which are worth looking through. I am especially fond of books dealing with mathematics. I love to look at pages of formulas, great masses of stuff which I have not wit enough to understand. But simply looking at it does me good. It makes me feel proud to know that I belong to a race which is capable of doing such wondrous things. And one of the books through which I love to look is a book on shades and shadows. That is the sort of book that an architect loves and an artist ponders. In these books I find that shadows can be computed. Under certain conditions shadows will be of a certain length and a certain breadth and a certain colour. It is possible for the whole problem to be worked out by applying the principles of geometry. Every shadow is cast according to law. If you could pick up a shadow from the street and carry it into a laboratory, you would find that it would not vary a hair's breadth from what it ought to be.

In this respect, all shadows are alike. We talk a good deal, in these days, about internationalism. There is an internationalism of shadows. All the shadows of the world constitute one great brotherhood. God has made of one all

the shadows of the earth.   The shadows in Asia are like the
shadows in Africa, and like the shadows in Europe, and like
the shadows of both the Americas, and like the shadows of
Australia, and like the shadows of all the islands of the sea.
All the shadows, in every land, are obedient to the same
laws, and these laws are the laws of the Eternal.

Here is a wonderfully interesting fact if you stop to ponder
it—that in all the thousands of shadows that play in our
New York streets, not one of them is disobedient to the law
of God.   These shadows are children of the Most High.
They play every day in our crowded streets.   The automo-
biles run over them, but they do not cry.   They are as death-
less as the Eternal, and every one is absolutely obedient to
the regulations of the King of heaven.   Look down Fifth
Avenue, some day, at the proper time, and notice the thousands of shadows.   Every lamp-post, every pole, every house,
every policeman, every moving pedestrian, every carriage,
every automobile, every horse, casts a shadow. What a wonderful thing that law is over all!   The rainbow is according
to law, and so is the Milky Way, and so is the shadow of the
little girl playing on Fifth Avenue.

I was riding down one of our avenues the other afternoon
with a friend, in his automobile, and I suspect that he did
not notice a single one of the many shadows over which he
passed.   I was looking at them all the way.   I noticed them
because this sermon was in my mind, and the sermon in my
mind made my eye keen to observe shadows.   That is one
of the purposes of a Nature sermon; it makes one's eyes keen
to things that would otherwise pass unnoticed.   All this summer through, not a person reading this sermon will fail to
notice more than once the play and beauty of the shadows.
A Nature sermon adds a province to the great kingdom of
our observation.

Since shadows, then, are the children of the Most High God, they are also His obedient servants. They fulfill His will, they do the thing for which they have been created. I have been looking through *The Psalm Book* during the last week, and I am convinced that it is defective. *The Psalm Book* has no proper appreciation of the ministry of shadows. The Hebrew poets are very sensitive to the beauty of many of the forces of Nature, and when they call upon the universe to worship God they name thunder and lightning and hail and sleet, snow, stormy winds, hills and mountains, trees and seas, sun and moon and stars, but there is no Hebrew poet so far as I can now remember who ever called upon the shadows to come into the Temple and lift voices of praise to the King of heaven. The Hebrew poet was impressed by the fact that the winds could be God's messengers, but he did not reach the point at which it was possible for him to see that the Divine Will can also be fulfilled by shadows. It will be worth our while to think of at least three of the ways in which shadows fulfill the will of God.

In the first place they enhance the beauty of the world. What would a picture be without shadows? Take the shadows out of any picture, and the picture is for ever spoiled. Take the shadows out of a landscape and it is flat and insipid. Why is it that noon is the least interesting of any portion of the day? Prose writers may talk of noon, but poets hardly ever do. There is nothing poetic in the noon. The poets sing of the morning and the evening, and the reason they sing of morning and evening is because the mornings and evenings are beautiful; and the reason mornings and evenings are beautiful is because mornings and evenings are the times of shadows. The day grows increasingly beautiful as it approaches its end. Life becomes increasingly rich as it draws to its close, and it is largely because the shadows are lengthening. As night comes on, the shadows become richer and more purple, and something passes into our soul which the noon cannot give. It is in the evening hours, before night comes, that the heart becomes more mellow and tender, and the angels of our better nature come out and sing.

Who does not love the twilight? Who does not love the deepening dusk? We speak sometimes of the gloaming. We love the gloaming because of the richness of the shadows. I have many times gone to Boston from New York on a morning train, and the journey is an interesting one because it carries one through the middle of the day. I am always impressed by the beauty of the country. But when I start for Boston at four or five in the afternoon of some lovely day in June, the whole country looks like fairyland because of the play of the shadows. There are shadows lying across all the streams, there are shadows on the surface of all the lakes. Every little pond throws a picture into your eye as you pass. The only perfect time to travel is during the hours immediately before the night falls. When the shadows are all around you, you feel that you are in a land of enchantment.

I had a friend, once, who was very sensitive to beauty. He was one of the most delicately organized men that it has ever been my fortune to meet. Like many another high-strung man it was difficult sometimes for him to sleep, and so in order to quiet himself it was his custom to walk up and down the avenue on which he lived, lined with great trees, and to study the shadows on the pavement. The moon has a wonderful fashion of turning pavements into silver and of using leaves as so many patterns with which to embroider beautiful figures on the silver. And my friend would walk up and down that avenue by the hour, feasting his soul on the beauty of the shadows in the street. And when he used

to talk to me about this feast of beauty I felt ashamed, for
I had walked that same avenue many times and had never
noticed a solitary shadow. In the presence of a man like
that I felt as much beneath him as I feel that my dog is beneath me. If it had not been for that man, the chances are
I should never have preached this sermon on shadows.

But shadows do more than simply minister to the æsthetic
part of our nature. They are genuinely useful. Long before
man had mechanical ingenuity enough to fashion a clock or
a watch, somebody had wit enough to make use of a shadow
by means of which to tell the time of day. Nobody knows
when the sundial was invented, but we can trace it back
through many centuries. Before the days of clocks and
watches men could tell how the hours were going simply by
watching the passing of the shadow round the dial. It is
said that even to the present time, travellers in the Arabian
desert who are not the owners of watches, find out what time
of day it is by the length of the shadow they cast upon the
sand. It is necessary for the pious Mohammedan to pray
at certain times each day, and instead of consulting a watch
he stands up against the sun and by the length of the shadow
which he casts upon the sand he finds out when the time of
prayer has come.

One of the most useful of all the shadows is the shadow of
the moon. When the shadow of the moon falls upon the
earth we call it an eclipse. There was a time when an
eclipse of the sun was one of the most terrifying of all phenomena. Men cried out in consternation when it came.
They were in an agony while it lasted. Not understanding
the cause of it they assumed it must be the creation of some
deity who was angry, so they quaked and shuddered as long
as the shadow lay across the land. But by and by, the

astronomers discovered the cause of the eclipse, and now it is counted one of the greatest blessings of which astronomers know. The eclipse of the sun is looked forward to with happy anticipation, and preparations are made months in advance in order to get the full advantage of it. Men are willing to travel halfway round the earth in order to get into advantageous positions so as to study the sun and the moon when the shadow falls. Many things about the sun we have learned because of this shadow, and many things about the moon, and also many things about the earth, which would have remained unknown probably for ever, if God had not ordained that now and then the moon's shadow should fall upon the earth. And so you might say that an eclipse is a great black bag full of secrets. Science has untied the string by which the mouth of the bag was closed, and has poured out the secrets before our eyes, so that we now know things about the sun and earth and moon of which the ancients never dreamed. All this knowledge came to us through a shadow.

Shadows are also fountains of refreshment. When man is hot and weary, he can cool his fevered brow by bathing in a shadow. Probably the greatest orator Israel ever produced was Isaiah. His literary style is stiff as cloth of gold; he is full of wondrous images, but not one of his images is more beautiful than this: "As the shadow of a great rock in a weary land." He is describing the Messiah, the long-looked-for man who is to bring relief to the weary world. In the Orient, they appreciate shadows as we do not do here. In Palestine, the sky is often without a cloud, and the sun beats down with pitiless intensity. In many parts of the land there are no trees and therefore no shelter from the sun at noon. In those regions the only shelter obtainable is that from a great boulder in the field. The weary traveller who has trudged along the dusty road, hour after hour, sees the boulder in the distance, and the very sight of it brings new courage to his heart. When at last he arrives at it, he throws himself down in its refreshing shadow, and out of that shadow receives strength sufficient to carry him to his journey's end. That is the picture that was in Isaiah's mind when looking down the years he saw the Messiah. He was to be like "the shadow of a great rock in a weary land."

Man is travelling across a desert, and the desert is sometimes blazing hot. Mankind is always on the point of withering, wilting, fainting because of the intensity of the heat of the day, and the Hebrew prophet thinking of the refreshment which the Messiah was going to bring, could think of no lovelier and more restful image than this: He shall be "as the shadow of a great rock in a weary land." There is a shadow which all of us are in love with—that is the shadow cast by the earth. Night is but a shadow, and at the end of every day, we creep round and throw ourselves down in this shadow and go to sleep. God takes the blanket of the night—and what is the blanket of the night but a shadow?—and this our heavenly Father spreads out over us and tucks it carefully in round us, and says to us, "Now, you may go to sleep." God giveth His beloved sleep, but we could not sleep so well were it not that He covers us with a shadow.

And if the shadow of night is our friend, we have a right to believe that the shadow of death is our friend. When the Hebrew poet thought of death it did not affright him. He knew it was only a shadow, and a shadow with refreshment in it. "Though I walk through the valley of the shadow of death, I will fear no evil," because the same God that is over us through the night will be with us in the midst of death. After we pass into that shadow we shall be refreshed.

Why do we have shadows? It is solely because of the existence of light. If there were no light there could be no shadows. The more light the more shadows. The intenser the light the deeper the shadows. One of the reasons why the Grand Canyon in Colorado is so indescribably beautiful is because of the richness of the shadows, and the richness of the shadows is due to the extraordinary luminosity of the heavens above the canyon. In that marvelous atmosphere the sun has a potency which he does not have in our sky, and the wonders he works far surpass any of the wonders which we know. Not a little of the indescribable loveliness of the canyon is due to the richness of the many-coloured shadows with which it is filled.

It was once my fortune to be in the city of Athens in the month of August. Athens, as you know, is a city of white. The Athens sky is often without a cloud, the sunlight flooding the streets of the white city producing a glare which almost dazzles the eyes. I was profoundly impressed, not only by the sunlight, but by the intensity of the shadows. There is a shadow which now lies across the world. It is a shadow cast by the late war. War is nothing new in this world. There has been war, so far as we know, from the beginning. But never has war cast a shadow comparable in blackness with the shadow which now lies on mankind. There have been military generals in all centuries—a thousand red-handed butchers have caused the earth to run red with blood, but never before has the world been under a shadow so deep and so awful as the shadow which oppresses human hearts to-day. How can you account for that? The only explanation is because of the intensity of the light. There is more of the light of the God of love that shines in the face of Jesus Christ than there has ever been in this world before. And it is because of the intensity of that light that we have the awful blackness of the shadow. The Indians once inhabited the land which is now ours. They were always fighting, but their wars cast no shadow because America in those days was dark. It is only because of the light that falls on us from the face of God's only begotten Son that war casts a shadow which lies like a beam of night across the tortured heart of the world.

And so there are two kinds of shadows: a shadow that refreshes and a shadow that oppresses, a shadow that enlivens and a shadow that deadens. Simon Peter cast a shadow that healed. That is a wonderfully interesting incident recorded in the fifth chapter of the book of *The Acts,* where we are told that people having invalids in their homes brought them out and laid them on beds and couches along the streets through which Peter was to pass, hoping that his shadow might overshadow them. Simon Peter stood between Jesus Christ and the world. The man who stands with the light of Christ on him will cast a shadow that has healing in it. You and I, if our attitude to the Eternal be right, will cast a shadow that will bring health and strength to all on whom it falls. I hope that this sermon may be a sermon casting a shadow (like that of Peter's) on you wherever you go, and that out of its shadow you may derive health and strength and peace.

IV

Harry Emerson Fosdick:
The Methods of a Master

Harry Emerson Fosdick is the master of life-situation preaching. No one has done as much to influence the modern emphasis on life-situation preaching as he has. In all the books that he has published he has not published one on preaching as such; fortunately, however, there are some brief statments he has made which give an insight into his thought and his methods. We shall quote from three that come from rather widely separated points in his career.

The first is from an article in *Harper's Magazine* in 1928. Here he states the purpose of such preaching. We referred to it in the introductory chapter.

> Every sermon should have for its main business the solving of some problem—a vital, important problem, puzzling minds, burdening consciences, distracting lives. . . . This endeavor to help people solve their spiritual problems is a sermon's only justifiable aim. The point of departure and of constant reference, the reason for preaching the sermon in the first place and the inspiration for its method of approach and the organization of its material should not be something outside the congregation but inside. Within a paragraph or two

. . . wide areas of any congregation ought to begin recognizing that the preacher is tackling something of vital concern to them. He is handling a subject they are puzzled about, or a way of living they have dangerously experimented with, or an experience that has bewildered them, or a sin that has come perilously near to wrecking them, or an ideal they have been trying to make real, or a need they have not known how to meet. One way or another they should see that he is engaged in a serious and practical endeavor to state fairly a problem which actually exists in their lives and then to throw what light on it he can.

Any preacher who even with moderate skill is thus helping folk to solve their real problems is functioning. . . .[1]

The second statement has to do with the preparation of a sermon. It appeared in 1932, as a chapter in a volume entitled *If I Had But One Sermon to Preach*. Here he gives us a view of the methods he follows in the preparation of his sermons.

Uniformly I am through with my manuscript on Friday noon. The next stage is one of the most important of all, for, fearful that in working out my subject I may occasionally have forgotten my object, and may have got out of the center of focus the concrete personalities who will face me on Sunday, I sit down on Saturday morning and re-think the whole business as if my congregation were visibly before my eyes, often picking out individuals, and characteristic groups of individuals, and imaginatively trying my course of thought upon them, so

---

[1]From "What's the Matter with Preaching," by Harry Emerson Fosdick, in *Harper's Magazine*, July, 1928. Used by permission.

as to be absolutely sure that I have not allowed any pride of discussion or lure of rhetoric to deflect me from my major purpose of doing something worth while with people. This process often means the elision of paragraphs that I liked very much when I first wrote them, and the rearrangement of order of thought in the interest of psychological persuasiveness.[2]

The final statement is from an article written for the journal, *Pastoral Psychology,* after his retirement from the active pastorate. He emphasized the same central purpose that he had stressed twenty-four years earlier. In this article, "Pastoral Counseling and Preaching," there was more emphasis upon the possibilities and results of such preaching.

Every sermon should have for its main business the head-on, constructive meeting of some problem which is puzzling minds, burdening consciences, distracting lives, and no sermon which so meets real human difficulty, with light to throw on it and power to win victory over it, can possibly be futile.

He referred to one particular problem with which he had worked years before. A young man had fallen victim to alcoholism and sought his help. After months of effort with the boy ended in success, he said it did something to his preaching.

From that day on the secret prayer which I have offered, as I stood up to preach, has run like this: "Somewhere in this congregation is one person who desperately needs what I am going to say; O God, help me to get at him!"

---

[2]From *If I Had But One Sermon to Preach,* by Joseph Fort Newton, copyrighted 1932 by Harper & Brothers. Used by permission.

Again, speaking of the results that can take place in life, he said,

> It is a great day in a minister's life, when having seen what miracles can be wrought by Christ's truth and power brought to bear on individual souls, he mounts his pulpit sure that a sermon, too, can be thus a medium of creative and transforming effects.[3]

Through the years he has combined an effective counseling program with great preaching.[4] In both preaching and counseling he utilized the best of modern psychology and mental hygiene together with the resources of religion.

It was difficult to select one sermon from the eight different volumes of sermons he has published. We have selected one because it is a bit different in emphasis, but any one of many might have been included. A mere listing of some of the titles gives an indication of his approach to preaching:

> "Handling Life's Second Best"
> "Getting Out of Us the Best that Is in Us"
> "The High Uses of Trouble"
> "When Life Goes All to Pieces"
> "No Man Need Stay the Way He Is"
> "How to Stand up and Take It"
> "When Great Events Make Common Tasks
>   Seem Trivial"
> "Finding Unfailing Resources"

Any one of these sermons might well be studied as an example of effective life-situation preaching.

---

[3] Reprinted by permission from the March, 1952, issue of *Pastoral Psychology.* Copyright 1952 by Pastoral Psychology Press, Great Neck, N. Y.

[4] See Introduction, *On Being a Real Person,* Harper and Bros., 1943, for a brief statement of his attitudes and experiences in pastoral counseling.

HANDICAPPED LIVES[1]

By Harry Emerson Fosdick

Our subject probably takes us all in. There may be some young, shining Apollo here who never has been aware of limitation, but one suspects not. At least, I never yet knew a man who on intimate acquaintance did not turn out to be dealing with handicaps.

Reading biography confirms the impression that all human beings are handicapped somewhere and that in no small degree the secret of the quality of any one's spiritual life depends on the way he is dealing with these limitations. In some ways, reading biography is disillusioning; we find our heroes far too human, with frailties and foibles like our own; but this compensating service biography does for us, constituting our heroes heroic still—it makes them all our companions in the handling of handicaps.

We thought, perhaps, that a scientist like Pasteur, upon whose titanic work modern medicine rests, must have had lusty health to labor with. We discover that he had a paralytic stroke at forty-six and was handicapped for life. We thought, perhaps, that a man like Henry M. Stanley, acclaimed of the whole world and buried from Westminster Abbey, must have had a grand heritage. We find he was brought up in an almshouse, and that his real name was not Stanley at all. We find Beethoven writing music although deaf and Milton writing poetry although blind, and we discover that in general the great work of the world has been

[1]From *The Power to See It Through*, copyrighted 1935 by Harper & Brothers. Used by permission.

done by handicapped people. They may have had faults and foibles like the rest of us but they had handicaps also, often far more severe than we have faced, and they dealt with them superbly.

How did they do it? What was the inward technique with which they handled limitations? Is there any one of us who does not need to learn that?

Biography in the Bible in no way differs from life stories outside. It confirms the universality of our problem. Take Paul's "thorn in the flesh," for example—"a messenger of Satan to buffet me." "I besought the Lord thrice," he wrote, "that it might depart from me. And he hath said unto me, My grace is sufficient for thee: for my power is made perfect in weakness."

No one knows what Paul's thorn in the flesh was. Epilepsy, eye trouble—many have been the guesses but no one knows. If Paul had been like some of us, some one would know. Think of writing all those letters and telling nobody the symptoms of his trouble! Ephesus, Colossae, Thessalonica, Corinth, and Rome would have been informed about it had Paul been like some of us. We know nothing, however, about Paul's trouble except that behind the scenes, like the rest of us, Paul had to handle a limitation that he prayed to escape, that he could not evade, that he had to settle down and live with somehow or other. Ah, Paul, handicapped man yet radiant in personality and successful in work, how did you handle it? What was the grace that was sufficient for you?

Often in churches we hear theological, ecclesiastical, and liturgical matters discussed as though the central problem of man's spiritual life somehow lay there. How far that is from the truth! How many of us really have the crux of our

spiritual problem in details of theology or theories of church
and liturgy? But we may be sure of one place where many
of us do have the central problem of our spiritual life, the
watershed from which the streams of life may flow to far-
dissevered destinies, and that is in the region of our handicaps.

Here is a boy born a cripple or crippled in early infancy;
he has grown up through his first years with no idea of what
has happened to him, but sometime in childhood it will
dawn on him that he is not like other children, that he has a
handicap. His spiritual problem will center in the way he
deals with that. Or here is a man whose parents did not
understand the critical importance of the emotional experiences of childhood, who now wakes up to discover that
something is wrong inside, that all his basic, habitual emotional reactions flow in channels of suspicion, distrust, fear,
anxiety, and vindictiveness, so that like a stream in endless
agitation he looks in envy at smoothly-flowing personalities
that can maintain a tranquil, deep, and even course. That
man's spiritual problem will center in the vicinity of his
handicap. Or here is a man who in youth had all the
natural ambitions of young manhood for success but who
now recognizes that he never will arrive at his desired goal.
He will never write the poetry or compose the music or
preach the sermons or hold the business positions that he
dreamed. Again and again he has stepped on the gas but
the speed is not in him. Nature did not equip him with
eight cylinders or with six—only four, and those none too
good. It is a crucial hour in that man's life when he stands
open-eyed before his handicap. Or here is a man who was
highly endowed and whose promising youth wakened in his
friends capacious expectations, but upon whom, like a beast
from ambush, an accident leaped, and now he must work

with crippled machinery. Again and again he has tried to
throw on the old power in the old way but it only burns out
the fuse. Somehow or other he must face his handicap

Moreover, there are some whose limitations lie in personal
relationships—a life that wanted love and missed it, a home
where marriage might have been a thing of beauty but was
a tragedy, a family where a child was greeted as a blessing
and became an inward agony, a household where death has
severed a tie that was the support and glory of the home.
Among the few things that are true of all of us is the fact
that each one has a handicap.

How, then, shall we deal with it? What is the technique?
Where is the grace that is sufficient for us?

In the first place, if we are to deal handsomely with our
handicaps we must at least have the grace to take, not a
negative, but a positive attitude toward them. The first
instinctive reaction toward a handicap is a negative attitude—rebellion or self-pity. How we rebel against our limitations! Why, we say, why, wanting to do some hard and
honest work in the world and to contribute something worth
while to life, should I be thwarted by this extraneous thorn
in the flesh? It was a common human failing that caused
Job's wife, when the crippling calamities fell on her husband, to advise him to curse God and die. Many a handicapped man has cursed God.

James Thomson, who wrote "The City of Dreadful
Night," for example, as a culmination to bereavement and
lost health had insomnia. His life was so clouded in gloom
that he, doubtless, was speaking in the words of one of his
characters:

> Who is most wretched in this dolorous place?
>   I think myself; yet I would rather be
>   My miserable self than He, than He
> Who formed such creatures to His own disgrace.

> The vilest thing must be less vile than Thou
> From whom it had its being, God and Lord!
> Creator of all woe and sin! abhorred,
> Malignant and implacable! I vow
>
> That not for all Thy power furled and unfurled,
> For all the temples of Thy glory built,
> Would I assume the ignominious guilt
> Of having made such men in such a world.

Well, such an attitude is natural if you have insomnia. But it is a poor technique for dealing with handicaps.

Many people, therefore, less vehement and tumultuous, try self-pity. They stroke their wounded spirits. Poor pussy, they say, poor pussy! If, they cry, I had not had this handicap, what a person I would have been! And so, drifting into imaginings of all they would have been and achieved, had not that handicap been there, they become very sorry for themselves that such a miserable thorn in the flesh should have kept them from so glorious a paradise. That is natural but it is not an efficient technique for dealing with limitations. A man must talk to himself more intelligently and courageously than that if he is to secure the grace that is sufficient for him.

For example, let a man say this to himself: Do you suppose that you are peculiar in having to handle second-bests? Few people get their first choice. To take a second-best and make something out of it is life. Whoever yet had a chance to live his life out under the ideal conditions he would have chosen?

Once when Ole Bull, the great violinist, was giving a concert in Paris, his A string snapped and he transposed the composition and finished it on three strings. That is life—to have your A string snap and finish on three strings. How many here have had to test that out! Some of the finest things in human life have been done that way. Indeed, so much the most thrilling part of the human story on this planet lies in such capacity victoriously to handle handicaps that, much as I should have liked to hear Ole Bull with all the resources of a perfect instrument at his command, if I could have heard him only once I should have liked to hear him when the A string snapped and, without rebellion or self-pity or surrender, he finished on three strings.

As soon as a man begins to take this positive attitude toward his handicaps, they begin to present themselves to him as opportunities—always challenging, sometimes fascinating. It is a good cook who, after the dinner has been burned, knows how to make a fine meal out of the left-overs, and a good cook will be challenged to try. When a man begins to see a possible technique here for dealing with his limitations, he begins to say to himself this: There are two kinds of elements in every situation, first, the things you cannot help—if the dinner has been burnt it is burnt; if the A string has snapped it has snapped—but, second, the things you can help—your attitude. Rebellion gets you nowhere. Self-pity gets you nowhere. But insight to see that something can be done with the second-bests and adventurous daring to try might be a handle to take hold of.

Some great stories have been told of people who did use that handle. Joseph did not want to be sent to Egypt. Betrayed by his brothers, sold into slavery, lied about by his master's wife and put in prison—that was a bad second-best. But that old story, born beside Bedouin campfires, now is naturalized beside modern radiators, because thus to face a second-best and make something of it, as Joseph did, is life.

Robinson Crusoe did not want to land on a desert island. Who wants a desert island even when he is tired of multitudinous New York? But while many a story rises and falls and passes away, that old tale retains its endless fascination because to be handed thus a second-best and make something of it is life.

Francis Parkman did not want poor eyesight. Who wants that? But one who knows his story reads his superb writings with an added thrill, seeing behind the printed page the manuscript with the wire screen across it where Parkman guided his pencil that he might write legibly.

So Paul did not want a thorn in the flesh. Temperamentally vigorous, active, aggressive—how he must have rebelled against it! "I besought the Lord thrice," he said, "that it might depart from me," and something tells me he lost count after that. But I suspect there are qualities of understanding and sympathy in Paul and a deep and moving music in some of the great passages of his epistles that never would have been there if he had not had to finish on three strings.

In the second place, if we are thus to take a positive attitude toward our handicaps, some of us will have to throw off a false sense of responsibility. The reason why many of us fret so at our limitations is that we keep comparing ourselves with others and wishing to be what they are or do what they do. We habitually measure ourselves by other people and assume a responsibility for being as fortunate, as useful, and as happy as they. Limited as I am, we say, I cannot be like So-and-So. It is a great day in a handicapped man's life when he makes up his mind that he has only one responsibility, not to be like anybody else but to handle his special situation as well as he can.

A consulting psychologist said some time ago that of the many cases of emotional maladjustment with which he deals, a large proportion were due to the fact that people would not accept themselves. Just so! We will not accept ourselves. We will not say what I am confident Paul in effect said: I, Paul, hereby accept myself with a thorn in my flesh and do hereby throw off all responsibility for dealing with any other Paul than myself, and having thus accepted myself with my handicap, which I cannot help, I will now fall to and see what good thing can be gotten out of myself in my special situation.

There are people here the inner tone of whose spiritual life and the outer result of whose practical endeavors would be transformed, if in that sense they would accept themselves.

Upon the other hand, see what we do. Born to be berry bushes and produce good berries, we lift anxious, envious eyes to apple trees with their larger-sized fruit, or, born to apple trees and produce good apples, we look with worried jealousy at maple trees with their more capacious shade, or, born to be maple trees, we are anxious because elm trees are taller and more graceful. We will not accept ourselves. Roll off, I beg of you, all responsibility for handling any other self or any other situation than the one you face.

I am well aware that this is not the ordinary tone of the pulpit. The preacher is all for putting responsibility on people. He ordinarily assumes that people are indifferent to their responsibility and proceeds to present to their acceptance the obligations that he thinks they ought to assume. But any man who works in confessional conferences with individuals learns that there are many people who never will get anywhere with their own problem or any one else's until they accept themselves. John Smith, he says, stop feeling responsible for being as fortunate or successful or happy or useful as some other man! That is not your business. You have been given this special field to till. Accept it. If the soil is thinner and the rocks more numerous and the prospects less promising than another's, that is simply life's problem which, in some degree, we all face. Stop looking over the fence and daydreaming about what you would do with another man's field. Your limitations are also your opportunities. Remember what Emerson's squirrel said to the mountain:

> If I cannot carry forests on my back,
> Neither can you crack a nut.

That spirit has brought out of small chances some of the most priceless results in human history.

If a man says he does not like himself, that is easily understood. There are millions of people with inside information about themselves who do not like themselves. Thomas Gray did not like himself. He had a melancholic temperament and he wanted a sanguine one. He wrote once to a friend, "Low spirits are my true and faithful companions." But when you read his "Elegy Written in a Country Churchyard," you feel that a priceless thing has been done with those somber moods that a merely jocund and hilarious temperament could not have achieved.

Diminutive edition of a man, William Wilberforce probably did not like himself. Boswell went to hear him speak once and said afterward, "I saw what seemed a mere shrimp mount upon the table; but, as I listened, he grew, and grew, until the shrimp became a whale." That shrimp of a man never had good health. For twenty years on doctor's orders he took opium to keep body and soul together and had the courage never to increase the dose. But more than any other Englishman he stopped the British slave trade, and as one stands in Westminster Abbey beside the grave of "The Attorney-General of the unprotected and of the friendless," one feels that that sensitive, suffering life translated itself into a persistent, unconquerable sympathy with downtrodden people that a lusty hulk of a man in perfect health probably never would have felt.

Do not despise your limitations. They are your opportunities. God will never judge us in masses. Each one of us will have a private examination. What did we do with our special situation? That is all. If you say, I am just as good as So-and-So, you will have missed the point. Perhaps So-and-So had much more severe handicaps. You should have done better. If you say, I am a failure, So-and-So beat me, you will have missed the point. God may say, Well done, good and faithful servant; you had a desperately difficult situation and you handled it superbly.

In the third place, if we are thus to take a positive and hopeful attitude toward our limitations, many of us must clearly perceive that however severely our outward service may be limited, we can always make a spiritual contribution to the world.

Some one has defined influence as the effluence of affluence. The most powerful and permeating influence is the aroma of rich and fragrant spirits, the effluence of affluence.

Now, handicaps, far from preventing the development of the influential quality, are almost the indispensable setting of it. Bring on your strong and shining Apollo who never had a handicap, who with integrated personality, fortunate circumstance, and physical health has lived untroubled by limitations, and, however energetic may be his active service in the world, there are some things he cannot do for us that

Helen Keller can. She is handicapped—blind, deaf, the doors shut on every side except the one door that even her handicaps can never shut, her chance to be a very radiant soul in a difficult situation. Being that, she does something to us which no shining Apollo can do.

The relationship, in this regard, between active and fortunate people on one side and handicapped spirits on the other is a fascinating study. Many of us may not be able to understand the argument or appreciate the antique beauty of "Paradise Lost" and "Paradise Regained," but one thing we all appreciate, the blind Milton sitting down to write them. That does something to us. Longfellow's translation of Dante may not by itself impress us. But when we learn that Mrs. Longfellow accidentally set her dress on fire, that Longfellow desperately but vainly tried to quench the flames, and that, after it all was over and Mrs. Longfellow had died, he sat down in his wifeless, motherless home to translate Dante to occupy his mind, and, what is more, did it beautifully, that does something to us.

How often we, with the shining sword of fortune and happiness still in our hands, tempted, for all that, to be laggard and cowardly, lift our eyes to see some man who has lost his sword, fighting with the scabbard, undaunted, high-spirited, unafraid—until we grasp our blades afresh and hew ahead! One cannot easily estimate the spiritual stimulus that comes into human life from handicapped people who have found grace sufficient for them.

My friend at a mid-western university tells me that in all his years there he never heard such cheering, not even at a football victory, as greeted a crippled boy carried in the arms of his companions across the platform on Commencement Day. Four years before, that boy had answered "Present" at the first roll call of his class. "Stand up!" said the professor. "I should like to, sir, but I have not been able to stand up since I was four years old." But, by being what he was in a difficult situation, that boy made such an impression on the university that, when his companions carried him up for his diploma, the great assemblage broke forth into such cheers as that college generation had not heard before.

Never despise your handicaps. They are an opportunity for a kind of spiritual service that lusty Apollos cannot render.

If you say that it takes great faith to live like this, you are right. You will not get this quality of life out of the atheistic cults some are trying to substitute for profound religion. If you say there are hours when you hate your handicaps, quite so! Even Christ prayed against the cross. *That* was a handicap. To die at thirty-three on a cross is a handicap. "If it be possible, let this cup pass away from me." He too prayed three times. But as it turned out in the end, no cross would have meant no Christ. That handicap was his most shining instrument. My friends, it was not the Greek Apollo, charioteer of the victorious sun, who won the world. It was the handicapped and crucified Christ.

V

Albert W. Beaven:
Preaching on the Home

Everyone recognizes the importance of the home; that is, almost everyone does. Perhaps we should say that everyone should recognize the importance of the home. Sociologists, psychologists, psychiatrists, educators, social workers are reminding us of it repeatedly. The significance of the home has been the subject of many books, countless articles, and innumerable speeches. Courses on marriage and the family are an accepted part of the curriculum of most colleges and universities. Special agencies have been established for the sole purpose of marriage counseling and family welfare. The church and the pastor also have a major responsibility in this matter. The church will reach some people that these specialists will never reach. The pastor has an emphasis to make on the sacredness of the home and on the place of religion in the home that is not often made by anyone else.

Every year for fourteen years Albert W. Beaven preached a series of what he called "Fireside Sermons" on the home. They proved to be very popular and the services were attended by large groups of people, both from the church and from the community. They were usually presented on Sunday evenings in the fall of the year. To supplement the sermons a "pastor's question box" period was often held following the service, sometimes in connection with a social hour which was designed to preserve a spirit of informality and to make it easier for the people to become acquainted.

He felt very deeply about the problems of the home and the responsibility of the church to help. "The Christian pulpit not only has a great obligation at this point," he said, "but a great opportunity. It can minister here with almost untold helpfulness. The place to help is before difficulties arise, and not after."[1]

As this statement indicates, he felt that one of the major tasks of the church was one of prevention, of providing such instruction and inspiration that problems do not arise. He found that this type of preaching had many values. It permitted him to say some things to the group that it would have been difficult to say to an individual or to a couple. It also enabled him to reach many people who would never have come for a private conference. Furthermore, he found that a valuable by-product was that it made the young people in his church conscious of the fact that he was interested in their homes and was willing to help them solve their problems, both before and after marriage. Thus it made an excellent background for any contacts with young people who came to him to be married.[2]

Each year he included some subjects that were of particular interest to young people before marriage and some that dealt with problems that arise in the making of a new home. Always there was a strong emphasis on the place of religion in the home. He dealt with such subjects as these:

> "Choosing a Mate"
> "The Greatest Problem in the World"
> "For Better or for Worse"
> "The Gentle Art of Living Together"
> "Some Parents I Have Met"
> "God and the Home"

---

[1]From *The Fine Art of Living Together,* by Albert W. Beaven, copyrighted 1942 by Harper & Brothers.
[2]See Beaven, *Putting the Church on a Full-Time Basis,* Harper & Bros., 1928, p. 94.

Some of these sermons have appeared in two volumes, *Fire-side Talks for the Family Circle* (Judson, 1928) and *The Fine Art of Living Together* (Harper and Bros., 1942). We have selected one from the second volume. Taken by itself it might be considered as rather incomplete, but considered as one in a series, it has real value.

PRACTICING THE "FINE ART" TOGETHER[1]

By A. W. Beaven

Life's greatest joy is reserved for the couple who learn the fine art of living happily with others. That it can be learned millions of people have proven; that many have not learned it millions of broken hearts testify. The ideal place to practice it and the most necessary place to use it is in wedlock.

The idea that love professed at the marriage altar will automatically solve all the difficulties between two people has been responsible for more heartache than anyone can compute. The fact is that all people who have ever been married have had their differences, and if they really learn the art of living together they have had to make readjustments that cost. The words spoken at the marriage altar do not change folks; they simply establish a new relationship. But in that relationship the two people have the strongest known human aid in solving the problem of their adjustments; namely, that marvelous emotion that we call love.

Each couple should face the fact that they will have some differences of opinion. The question is not whether they will have these differences, but what they will do with them when they come. These can either be a source of irritation and permanent trouble, if handled unwisely, or, if handled wisely, they can be an open doorway into a better understanding of each other. Nowhere does the advantage of a genuine Christian spirit come more into evidence.

[1]From *The Fine Art of Living Together*, copyrighted 1942 by Harper & Bros. Used by permission.

At one time I sent out a questionnaire to over seven hundred and fifty couples whom I had united in marriage. In answer to the question: "What, in your judgment, is the greatest element making for happiness in home life?" the largest number said: "Religion lived daily in the home." By definition in the questionnaire this involved those attitudes and practices in daily living which grow out of an honest desire to be Christian in deed as well as word. Such religion enables the couple to build a machinery that will actually change differences of opinion into assets. Let us see the situation as it stands when the differences which are common to family life occur. Ordinarily, the different point of view is taken because of different training or different desires, and it is not a satisfactory solution of the situation for one to be able to force the other to come to his or her point of view.

When Both Lose

Let us realize at the outset that the real objective in married life is not to have the man or the woman "the boss," nor to have one do all the giving in while the other always has his or her own way. If either one always forces the other to give in in a contest of opinions then both have lost. The art of living together is learned when each sees the other's point of view and respects it. The ultimate decision must come after a consideration that has given both a fair deal. Otherwise, even though the one seems to win, the quarrel still stands there and will remain in the heart of the one who gave in, to cause bitterness and heartache. This will produce an explosion later.

When Differences Help

No difference is solved permanently unless it is solved rightly. This is why religion is so practically helpful. The Christian religion includes the insistence that whatever we would that other people should do to us we should do that very thing to them. The Christian ideal insists that we try fairly to see the other's point of view It demands that we should settle things, not by resorting to force, either that form of force known as stubbornness or force shown in the ability to wear the other down by talking and nagging, or the use of any other of the weapons of human autocracy, but it insists that the primary question is this: "What is right and fair and just?" The machinery that will enable two people to agree as to what is fair and to accept it as a valuable mechanism for any home.

Nor is such machinery hard to create. Suppose two people who love each other have something over which hard feeling has arisen. It will only make matters worse to discuss it before others, or even to discuss it when they are tired or irritated. Let them make it a point to say as little as possible in public but reserve for the quiet of their own room a full and frank discussion. If that conversation can be conducted in the mood described in the fifth to the eleventh verses of the thirteenth chapter of First Corinthians, we doubt whether any quarrel could long survive.

One part of this machinery for dealing with the whole matter of differences of opinion is an understanding of the psychology of argument. In any argument, while the first person is speaking the second person is so busy thinking what he will say in rebuttal that he almost never fully listens to the other's point of view. Argument usually strengthens each in his own opinion and closes the mind to the other's reasoning. Really extended argument between married couples seldom settles anything. As a substitute let us suggest this method. In the quiet of their own room let one state fully his or her own point of view without interruption, and then let the other one have a chance to speak his or her point of view just as fully and without interruption. In this way the real ends to be gained can more easily be seen because each can fairly get a view into the other person's feelings and can clearly see what is behind the difference. It is no uncommon experience for any one of us to find under such conditions that what we interpreted to be stubbornness was genuine contention for values that it would have been tragic for both to lose. Such a method as this enables both to pick out what is worth while in the two points of view and save it and usually the part that is unworthy is seen in equally true perspective. This is using religion in a practical way.

The School of Love

What a tragedy it is when people fail to realize early in married life that the thing which counts most is the ability to make each other happy. It makes little difference how many other girls a man can be pleasant to and interest; if he cannot interest his own wife and make her happy the other things count little. It makes little difference how attractive a girl can be out in company, or how fascinating she is to others, if at home she constantly says and does things that irritate her husband and keeps the atmosphere of the home one of contention and faultfinding, she is a failure as a wife.

The art of living together is an art that must be learned. If it is worth while for a girl to study to become a stenographer or a teacher or for a man to prepare to be a salesman or a doctor, is it not worth while to discipline ourselves and by determined effort to learn this art of living with each other happily? The first two or three years of married life can have no objective finer than the learning of this art. If it is learned the machinery for taking care of all sorts of difficulties has been erected and can be used. If it has not been learned one matter after the other that has been argued about comes to be taboo because whenever it is touched hard feeling is engendered. In some homes into which one goes there are things by the score that can hardly be mentioned without creating a tension. Differences of opinion arise, quarrels follow, these are not settled, they are hung up as it were on the walls of the room, ready to be taken down and used as the excuse for a new controversy whenever anybody mentions them. No home that we can go into is more unhappy for the two who constitute it, or the friends who visit it, than the one that has no machinery set up for taking care of its differences of opinion. Explosions take place in public, hard words and pent-up feelings are always breaking forth and it is no wonder that under strains of this kind living together ultimately becomes impossible. The man spends long years in preparation for his life work that he may be able to properly support his home. The girl often takes a course in domestic science that she may know how to take care of the home. Why should not every couple definitely and consistently take a course in the art of living together happily, taught by that majestic Teacher, the Christ? Surely any two people who love each other and will give Him and His spirit a fair chance in their lives can become adepts in this gentle art of creating a happy home life.

VI

Leslie Weatherhead:
Preaching in a Time
of Crisis

Leslie Weatherhead, well-known pastor of the City Temple in London, has gained an almost world-wide audience through his numerous writings and lecture tours. He is recognized as one of the pioneers in the study of the relationship of psychology and religion. He conducts a "psychological clinic" in connection with his church in London in which he uses all of the help of medicine and psychotherapy along with the resources of religious faith. In addition to his writings on the relationship of psychology and religion, he has published many volumes of sermons that have had a wide circulation in this country. One of the most significant was a volume that was produced during the most difficult days of World War II. It is an excellent example of preaching in a time of national crisis. The entire volume was entitled *This Is the Victory*. We have chosen a sermon on "Patience" which was included in a group of sermons on "Faith's Allies" in which he also spoke of Beauty, Humor, Hope, and Truth. There are frequent references to the conditions of the day from which the sermons come. A few paragraphs from the preface of the book give some of the background and thus more meaning to the sermon.

I should like this Preface to provide some kind of background from which this book emerges. As I write these words in the autumn of the year of our Lord in 1940, my house in London trembles with the vibration caused by the firing of guns, the explosion of bombs, and the falling of houses. Last night my elder son and I went on duty for the local air-raid warden in order that he might get what chance there is of a night's sleep. The siren, warning the city of imminent air raids, wailed its melancholy message at dusk, and the "all-clear" signal went just before six the next morning. All through the long, hideous night the din went on. In my neighborhood five people were killed near one end of the road and three near the other. Night after night this is what is happening in London. Thousands are homeless. In one month seven thousand have been killed and ten thousand injured. Seven hundred of the killed were children under sixteen. Seven hundred of the injured were also children. Every evening multitudes take a three-halfpenny ticket on the underground railway, and, admitted to the platform, stay there all night. If they queue up early enough to get sufficient space, which some do long before midday, they lie down. If not, they stand up all night, and then, hollow-eyed and weary, go to work the next morning. . . .

The work of the minister of religion can easily be imagined. He must "carry on" as far as possible, though daily his difficulties increase. People need God as never before. Yet transport difficulties make both the minister's visiting and a journey to churches in Central London a matter of hours. And people are so starved of sleep, so tired of journeys, that who can blame them if they stay at home? After dark it is definitely foolish to be out unnecessarily. The antiaircraft barrage means that shrapnel falls like hail. Every Londoner has two or three pieces on his mantlepiece, picked up near his home or in his gutters. . . .

All ministers find their visiting heartbreaking. I recall an afternoon in which I visited a paralyzed boy, a family of ten with hardly a room left to them by the fires that raged all round them, two maiden ladies whose little business has almost come to an end through war, and a girl with both feet trapped by her falling house. Another girl from my church, bravely doing her duty as an A.R.P. warden, has had her arm blown off by an explosion outside the warden's post.

My telephone rings. A doctor, a member of my church and a Harley Street specialist, asks whether I will go to such and such a hospital as soon as possible. A girl is lying there badly injured. Her sister was killed last night. Her mother has not yet been found, though men have been digging and searching ever since the house was demolished. Her father is dead also. I must try to comfort her.

So day follows day in agony, sorrow, and suffering. People are very brave. There is no doubt about that. And they believe Britain will win, though they wonder what meaning the word "win" will have. They keep a smile as near the surface as they can, and they keep a stiff upper lip for the sake of those who have to live with them. But I cannot help feeling that underneath is a sense of futility and bewilderment not far from a kind of secret despair. "Where is it all going to end?" they ask.[1]

It was against such a background that he preached on the theme of patience. No doubt many people who heard him gained new perspective and new hope. In a sense, this sermon is dated because of the specific situation that it was prepared to meet; however, in another sense, it is timeless, for all men need patience in all experiences of life.

[1]From *This Is the Victory* by Leslie D. Weatherhead. Copyright 1941 by Whitmore & Stone. By permission of Abingdon Press.

PATIENCE[1]

By Leslie Weatherhead

One of the reinforcements of faith which we need most is patience. It is good to have the glimpse of purpose and plan which faith gives us, but what a lot of patience we need to toil along the road before the goal is reached!

One of the most thrilling passages in Browning's "Paracelsus" is surely that in which he tells how with flagging feet he toiled onward, the goal out of sight, and then how a vision of the city buoyed him up and sent him on with reinforced faith, patiently to struggle until he arrived.

> I remember well
> One journey, how I feared the track was missed,
> So long the city I desired to reach
> Lay hid; when suddenly its spires afar
> Flashed through the circling clouds; you may conceive
> My transport. Soon the vapors closed again,
> *But I had seen the city,* and one such glance
> No darkness could obscure:

Then comes the need of patience and he adds,

> Nor shall the present,
> A few dull hours, a passing shame or two,
> Destroy the vivid memories of the past.
> I will fight the battle out; a little spent
> Perhaps, but still an able combatant.

[1]From *This Is the Victory* by Leslie D. Weatherhead. Copyright 1941 by Whitmore & Stone. By permission of Abingdon Press. Because of the length of this sermon it has been slightly abbreviated. In no wise has the meaning been changed.

We need that patience now. The war drags on, and I know that I am writing about something that is relevant to our need, at any rate; the black-out nights, the dislocation of our ordinary activities and interests, perhaps the invasion of our homes by other folk, the strain of nightly bombardment, the lack of sleep, the vague fear and fretfulness which attacks our minds have meant for us a new need of patience.

This war has rightly been called a war of nerves: the insecurity of our job, perhaps; the sense of daily and nightly danger; the strain, day after day, of wondering what is happening to our loved ones, what may happen to them—indeed, what may happen to us all. All these things are putting a big demand on all our hearts.

I think that our own patience will be maintained better if we can consider the patience of God. I know that some of God's ministries are swift in their action. We think of the lightning, the earthquake, the tornado, and the flood. These things descend upon man with terrific speed and violence, and there is much about them that we do not understand. But when our minds turn to the creative purposes of God, we find that the rule is that God works very slowly, very patiently. I suppose it is because he knows what he is doing, how it is all going to turn out, and that all his patience will prove worth while. . . .

I remember some years ago, before I lived in London, taking an appointment on the south side of the River Thames and coming back to London to stay at a hotel for the night. I happened to walk along the northern bank of the river about midnight. In imagination I tried to see that great river in the far-off olden days, when it flowed through the meadows, silently down to the sea. I can't reproduce here the spirit, the atmosphere, of that night. It was a lovely, clear, frosty, dry, starlit night, and London was sinking down to quiet and rest, and I thought, as many have thought before me, if that old river could talk what a lot it could say to us all.

I thought of the days when the river flowed through the wooded valleys and quiet meadows down there by the Strand and out through the marshes and into the sea. As I passed, on the Embankment, Cleopatra's Needle—that monument that goes back into the dim mists of history—I remembered Sir James Jeans saying that if you stuck a postage stamp on the top of Cleopatra's Needle, then the thickness of the stamp compared with the height of Cleopatra's Needle would give you an indication of the length of time men had been on the earth compared with the time during which there had been an earth. I have read that if one divided the history of this world into 7,000 equal parts, then during the first 6,999 there would be no sign of man.

> This fine old world of ours is but a child
> Yet in the go-cart. Patience! Give it time
> To learn its limbs: there is a Hand that guides.

How patiently God prepared for man! Some tell us that he took two thousand million years to prepare a home for man.

I like to think of all those processes that make it possible for a gaily colored butterfly to develop from the caterpillar, emerge from its chrysalis, and rise up into the sunshine. Yet in one day that tiny fragment of beautiful life has lived its span, fulfilled its purpose, and passed away. All that patient preparation for so small a thing, so short a life, makes me very ashamed of my impatience.

There is no adequate human illustration of that kind of thing. The nearest, perhaps, is the patient building of a great cathedral, such as that at Liverpool. The architect, who was just a young man of twenty-one when his plans were accepted, dimly hopes, if he is spared, that the cathedral may be somewhere near completion before he dies. The only other human illustration that attracts me is that lovely story of the American tourist who went to Oxford. He was strolling through the gardens of one of the colleges and said to the gardener, "How do you get these lawns like this?" The old gardener looked at him and said, "Well, sir, you see, we just waters them and mows them and rolls them, and waters them and mows them and rolls them, and waters them and mows them and rolls them for eight hundred years, and then they are like that." And the American said, "Well, I guess I had better go back to New York and begin."

When we think of those processes which have paved the way for beautiful things, how the patience of God stands out against our impatience! It is our impatience which makes it seem to us that God doesn't answer prayer. There cannot be such a thing as an unanswered prayer. If you were a father and your little child tugged your coat and said, "Daddy, I want . . ." you would not push him away. You would not avert your face and look the other way and assume a stony stare. You might not be able to give him what he wanted, but you would pick him up in your arms and love him. How stupid it must really be to talk about unanswered prayer! If God is a Father and God is love and you are his child, there cannot be such a thing as a refusal to answer. I am sure this patient, loving God is whispering to our hearts, "Wait! wait!" That is a very hard lesson for man to learn. God is more patient than man dreams credible. Man's refusal to believe in God's patience, in my view, accounts for the form which the story of the Flood took. Some local calamity there probably was.

But it was incredible to godly men in those days that the God who was holy and omnipotent could put up any longer with man's sins and futilities. So an ancient happening became a legend which taught that God just wiped the slate clean of dirty human nature, "drowned the lot" save a select few, and started again. That is man making God in his own image, man making a mental concept of an impatient God because he didn't believe God could possibly bear with men any longer.

When I look at my own heart with its incessant appeals for forgiveness and its endless new beginnings, I am amazed that God can stand me any longer—I am still more surprised that he can stand some people I know. Perhaps it was an inability to accept the thought of God's infinite patience that led the Calvinists into some harsh doctrines. The Calvinists tried to understand why nine-tenths of the people did not care for God; so they said it must be that God does not will to save them. They are not the chosen ones; God has no time for them—as we say. "Why doesn't God *make* man repent?" asked the Calvinists; and since there seemed to be no answer, then, said the Calvinists, it must be that he does not want them. So, out of their own impatience they made a false mental image of God as dangerous as a false metal image of God.

I remember hearing my predecessor in Leeds, the Rev. A. E. Whitham, who now has gone into the great silence, say, "If I were God I think I would have a brass plate on the door; at any rate I would make people's ears burn, I would teach them to show me due respect." But I am glad he was not God though I loved and admired him! The real God does not strive or cry or let his voice be heard in the streets. He does not hustle men into decisions or hurry their mental processes. Love is very patient, very kind.

Theodore Parker said, "The trouble is that God is not in a hurry, and I am." That is the trouble with a lot of us. Many of us are saying in our hearts, "If I were God I would teach Hitler where he got off. I would not let him do this, that, and the other. Why doesn't God do something?" The poet Whittier said as he fought for freedom for the slaves, "I confess when I think of the atrocities of slavery, I am almost ready to call fire from Heaven."

I think there was a time when even Jesus was tempted to be impatient. As I try imaginatively to watch him out there in the desert after the baptism, when he knew that he stood in a unique relationship with God, out there in the great silence, as he watched the great planets wheel in the sky, as he lived among wild beasts for over a month in prayer and self-discipline, I catch a glimpse of that patience in which he won his soul. He was thinking out his program. He did *so* want to get the ear of the people. What was the way to do it? The flat stones looked like the loaves his mother made, and as he saw them he said, "Yes, my people are starving; my people won't listen to me yet. If I bring in a new order of things, so that there is food for these hungry people to eat, then they will listen to me." He could have brought about social reform. It would have been a quick way to get the ear of the people, but it did not fit in with God's way. It was a short cut. It was buying men's allegiance with bread. So he put it behind him. You cannot change hearts by providing bread, and there is no progress without changed hearts.

The inner voice of impatience said, "You could float down from the pinnacle of the temple, you could do wonderful things; nothing arouses the enthusiasm of people so much as a person who will work magic." Then, as he thought it all out in the light of the patience of God, he knew that miracles must never be worked to make a short cut to men's hearts. So he put that behind him too. No miracles were worked to make men say "Isn't he wonderful?" You cannot change men's hearts with magic. They will be amazed and follow from curiosity and then go on as before. And there is no progress without changed hearts.

The voice of impatience tried again: "Never mind, the country is ripe for revolution; lift your finger and a thousand men will bring their swords. You could claim all the kingdoms of this Jewish world. They are looking for a King." Then he knew that that would not do either. You cannot buy men with patriotism if you want them for God, because God's kingdom is bigger than that and takes in all kingdoms. God's kingdom is the kingdom of the changed heart. Nationalism is frequently its greatest enemy.

There was something born in the desert that day—a new patriotism, the idea of a greater kingdom, where *all* should be brothers and *all* the children of God. And that is going to take a long time; it is going to take all the patience of God, for he must wait for the tardy co-operation of men. So Jesus put it away from him. He knew there were no short cuts. In patience he had won his soul.

Do you remember the picture of the man sowing tares in an enemy's field, and how the human remedy was immediate action to root them up? But Jesus said, "Let them grow together until the harvest."

Do you remember this word about God? "For he maketh his sun to rise on the evil and on the good, and sendeth rain on the just and on the unjust."

Do you remember the day when the disciples were with Jesus in a Samaritan village, and the Samaritans would not

listen to him, and the disciples said, "Lord, wilt thou that
we bid fire to come down from heaven, and consume them?"
But Jesus said, "You don't understand." They didn't understand the patience of God; and all through the Gospels
it is the same story.

Do you sometimes at a communion service shut your eyes
and go back in imagination to that long, low upper room,
and see the lamp swaying in the evening breeze, and the
disciples reclining at the table only eighteen inches high?
Do you feel the sense of indescribable sorrow? Do you almost hear Judas' sandals scraping over the floor as he leaves
and makes for the doorway? If those disciples had known
what he was going to do, they would have stood between
him and the door, even killed him, rather than let him do
what he was going to do; but Jesus said, "What you are
going to do, do quickly." How patient Jesus is! Those
disciples could not take in the thoughts of Christ about his
kingdom. They wanted quick action, quick results. They
thought that there would be a king reigning and they themselves on thrones around him. Do you remember how the
mother of two of them was so anxious about those thrones
that she wanted one of her sons to be on the right hand
and the other on the left when the King came in his kingdom? But when he came in his kingdom, his throne was a
cross, and on his right and on his left were two thieves.
What a long way round to a kingdom! But that is the way
he took us. He is taking us that way again, and we must
share his patience.

In an old-fashioned novel the heroine asks her uncle this
question, "What does one end by doing when all the best is
taken away from one, when life has grown trivial, stunted,
and narrow; when the sun of one's happiness is set?" And
here is the wise answer of an old man: "After a time, Polly,

not at once—that would be asking too much of poor human nature—but after a time, my dear, one lights a candle called Patience, and guides one's footsteps by that."

Well, if we are wise, and are determined to come out of this war spiritually victorious, we shall add to our faith patience. We shan't wait too long before we light such a candle. For this is the day of black-outs in more senses than one. When Earl Grey, then Sir Edward Grey, Britain's Foreign Secretary, saw in the summer of 1914 that war was inevitable, he stood at the window of the Foreign Office and said, in a voice that no one who heard it will ever forget, "The lights are going out in Europe." I wonder what that lovely soul would say today? Even to youth I would say: "Light your candle. You have started out to train for a career in hope of a joyous life, full of service to the community; and now your progress, perhaps your very existence, is threatened. Light a candle of patience." To many in middle life with a reasonable sense of security I would say: "Light your candle. The security of anything in this world is overshadowed by a great darkness." To those in old age I would say: "Light your candle, for the light of a candle of patience lit at the burning love of Christ may be the only light for you at eventide."

We all need patience. The nervous tension caused by war makes us jumpy and irritable. Trifles at which we should have laughed in the old carefree days can upset us out of all proportion to their importance. We hurt even our dearest by a sharp word or cutting remark.

The chaotic transport, which used to run so smoothly and up to time, doesn't breed patience. The waiting, the rushing for bus or tube, having to fight a good fight to get in at all—these activities make us impatient with others, hectic and short-tempered.

The awful, grim struggle, to which at present we can see no end, makes us impatient. We view the cost in men, in money, in nervous health with dismay. We wonder whether ever again will come the old, lovely, happy, carefree days we once enjoyed. . . .

No wonder we pray for patience. . . .

The word "patience" . . . is not a passive word. It is a dynamic word. "Let us *run* with patience," says the author of the letter to the Hebrews, not "Let us sit with patience." Patience is often pictured with folded hands. Not so in the New Testament. The sentence of Paul, "In your patience ye shall win your souls," is translated by Dr. Moffatt thus: "In your *perseverance* ye shall win your souls."

Luke uses the word in the elucidation of the parable of the sower. The seed on the good ground brings forth fruit with patience, and bringing forth fruit involves—does it not?— activity, taking something from the rain, the sun, the soil, and turning it into fruit. Every vine knows how to turn the water into wine. Yet, in spite of activity, growth is a matter of patience. You may fume and fret at the long winter, but you can do nothing to hurry the spring. Activity and patience are not opposites, but complements.

It is of God's ordaining, this slowness in the *growth* of the most worth-while things. The sudden conversion? Yes, but the finest souls know that while they are at the end of the wandering, they are only at the beginning of their journey. The sudden flash of lightning may rend the mountain peak and leave a scar, but that sudden cleft only provides the opportunity for tiny seeds to find lodgment. Day after day mountain mists must kiss the hard crag with their cool, fertilizing breath; a whole season of rain and shine must pass before the cleft can fill with those tiny wild flowers—the mountain pansy, the vetch, the pimpernel, which the mountain wears as proudly as a woman the gems of her beloved.

Everyone who has learned a language—including his own —knows what I mean by patience which is active as well as passive. Everyone who plays an instrument well knows how much work and how much patience are needed. Everyone who has *learned* to do anything well, from running a home to a country, knows the stern demand on patience.

We shan't expect to escape in our religious life, shall we? For myself, I know that I've done nothing yet but make the poorest kind of start, with faltering and failure and many turnings back, but I am determined on one thing: I won't give up. If he were any ordinary kind of Leader, he would have given me up long ago, but his patience and love are far greater than mine. I have his promise: "I will never leave you nor forsake you. He that cometh after me I will in no wise cast out." I'm going to cling to those promises. I want to hold on until, in my own life and that of this great nation, I can see God working out his plans.

And when I'm tempted to be impatient with my own progress and tempted to give the whole thing up, I'm going to take a look at Jesus, and remember that if I miss—what I believe to be the most wonderful experience a human being can ever have—a saving experience of his love, it won't be his fault, but mine. So, I'll run with patience, looking unto Jesus, the Author and Perfecter of faith.

I'll take a look at Jesus, too, when I'm tempted to be impatient with others. They can't try me a tenth as much as I try the patience of Christ. And so often, I find, I'm impatient with people because I just don't understand what is happening in their hearts and minds.

Here's a true story to illustrate what I mean. The chef on a luxury liner used to delight the passengers by making the cakes for tea and the ices for dinner in the most attractive shapes. One might find a little cake like a basket of fruit. One might find an ice-cream in the form of a model of the ship. One day the little cakes were not as "cute" as usual, and an American girl complained accordingly. She didn't know that while the vessel slipped through the sunny seas it was taking the chef further and further from a wife who was desperately ill. The American spoilt darling didn't know that when the chef was trying to do better in consequence of the complaint that was passed on to him, he got a wireless message to say that his dearest was dead.

I knew of a school in the north in which every boy who was late was caned without being given any opportunity of offering an explanation. One morning a master severely thrashed a lad for lateness, only to find afterwards that the latecomer had been at the pit head all night waiting for news of his brother who was trapped underground in a coal mine and who was subsequently brought out dead. The story—which I verified—came to me when I was engaged in a press campaign against caning in schools which cost me much opposition and abuse. One's blood boils at the incident, but I wonder what our own impatience has cost others—and God!

I'll take a look at Jesus when I'm tempted to lose patience with God and say to him, "Why did you ever make such a world if you can't run it better than this?" "God is in Heaven, thou upon earth; therefore let thy words be few." Yes, there's wisdom there. All this sorrow and loss and worry and pain. . . . But he *knew* it was possible, that it would come—and he went on building and planning and trusting men.

Two dear friends of mine, an elderly man and his wife, were going with my sister to see Liverpool Cathedral. As they examined the exterior, the old lady said, as she poked at the stone with her umbrella, "I think they have chosen the wrong kind of stone. It's pretty, but it's too soft. It won't last." To which, with a twinkle in his eye, her husband answered, "Yes, dear; but, you know, I expect the architect thought of that!"

How we complain about God's world! Why didn't he do this and that? We forget that nine-tenths of its misery has come because man has gone wrong at this point or that. And for the rest, and indeed for the possibility of all the sorrow and suffering in all the world, we may say reverently, "The Architect of the universe thought of that."

When I look at the Cross, I say to myself very quietly—and a strange awe and hush comes upon me—"He thought of that." He knew it would cost that. And he went on because he had enough patience to believe that it was worth even that. And he who hung there—he who, so pure and innocent, might have railed at God and called the universe a failure, a devilish fraud, a foul obscenity—called God *Father,* and died in unbroken peace. And all the saints in their own way, and so many of them at cost of everything that human lives count dear, followed that lead.

We are just to walk quietly along each day's road with persevering patience, looking unto Jesus, and leaving responsibility to God. He has thought of everything that can happen to us. You may have every reason for impatience. An income cut down yet again. Little children perhaps thrust upon you even while your own are far away. A difficult husband—as my wife has. A sense of insecurity in your job and the awful strain of what may never come, the threat to your dear ones, your homes and lives and existence. . . . He knoweth the way that you take. He has thought of that!

None of us will ever have to face a situation which has not been faced by those who love Christ. In imagination I sometimes see the roof of the City Temple roll back, and a multitude of the heavenly host praising God with us and looking down on us with great love and with shining eyes, hoping desperately that we shan't—in our day and generation—let things down.

"Therefore let us also, seeing we are compassed about with so great a cloud of witnesses, lay aside every weight, and the sin which doth so easily beset us, and let us run with patience the race that is set before us, looking unto Jesus the author and perfecter of our faith"—the faith in which alone the spirit finds its victory. "This is the victory that overcometh the world, even our faith."

VII

Walter Russell Bowie:
Interpreter of Scripture

Walter Russell Bowie is noted both as a preacher and a teacher of preachers. For thirty-one years he served as a pastor. Since 1939, he has been a professor of homiletics. He has had the honor of delivering the Lyman Beecher Lectures on Preaching at Yale. For many people, however, he is best known as an interpreter of Scripture. He has taken the best of the findings of biblical scholarship and combined it with deep devotional insight, and thus has made the Bible become alive and helpful in this modern age. It is with this thought in mind that we include him in this series. He is representative of those men who have used the Bible to give understanding and meaning to life.

For Walter Russell Bowie the Bible is the great source book for the understanding of life. In his own words, he says,

Through the words of the printed Bible, great souls are speaking, souls who have been face to face with the old, yet ever new, problems of the same sort of experience with which we deal. They, like ourselves, have been confronted with difficulties which they could not seem to batter down, surrounded with perplexities which they could not get through, isolated in a moral loneliness in which they seemed to find no comradeship upon which they could lay hold. But these great figures into whose presence the Bible leads us prevailed. They were in sore straits, but they did not stay there. They passed through their narrow place into that fulfilment of life to which their faith and courage ultimately found an open way. Communing in our thought with them, insensibly but surely we begin to lose our unrest. They stand in a spiritual calm. About them is none of that atmosphere of shared disquiet which our living human friends cannot help in some measure reflecting from ourselves. These figures in the Bible have attained to certainty. They bear that witness which can only be borne by those whose record is assured, and yet they do not speak with any aloof detachment. It is as though they shared with us the fellowship of their most real experiences. Back from the heights to which they have advanced, they come to walk with us as comrades of the spiritual way. "No road on which your conscience tells you you ought to walk is at length impossible, they say. No work which your conscience tells you to take up is so difficult that it cannot finally be well done. No odds against you are so heavy that you cannot battle through." Thus they speak, these great souls of the Bible, and, listening, we take courage and go on.[1]

In his lectures on preaching he says that the Bible should be the preacher's greatest resource. It should be "the supreme area for a preacher's thinking and for his preaching." This does not mean that he should ignore other means of understanding his people. A knowledge of the Bible alone

---

[1]From *When Christ Passes By*, by Walter Russell Bowie, copyrighted 1932 by Harper & Brothers. Used by permission.

is not enough to guarantee that one preaches with understanding. It must be coupled with an understanding and concern for the people in his congregation. So, along with his urging that men should know the Scriptures, he says,

> On the days when he is getting the sermon ready, every thought that passes through his (the preacher's) mind ought to be warmed by the recollection of the people who on that next Sunday morning may be listening to what he says. It is well that at some time he should go into the church and kneel there in one of the pews and remember those who will be sitting there. Here in one place will be a businessman, burdened and often bewildered by the difficulty of keeping his business from being a failure and at the same time keeping himself a Christian. Here will be a woman bringing in her heart some secret wound of domestic wretchedness. Here will be the young man undecided whether to resist or welcome some hot temptation. Here, seated side by side, will be two who have fallen in love and before whom life seems to be opening into the wonder of new romance. Here they are, these different personalities with their different joys and sorrows, their opportunities and their needs. What can the message he plans to preach on Sunday be made to mean to them?[2]

If he is to speak to these people in this manner, along with knowing the Scripture, Dr. Bowie says that he must "know his people one by one."

[2]From *Preaching*, by Walter Russell Bowie. By permission of Abingdon Press.

The sermon that we have selected is one from a series of sermons on "Great Men of the Bible."   It is a sermon based on the experience of the Apostle Paul. It not only gives insight into the career of this great biblical scholar, but also speaks to a problem that is present in almost every life.

GREATNESS UNDER DIFFICULTIES[1]

By *Walter Russell Bowie*

*I know both how to be abased, and I know
how to abound.*
— Philippians IV: 12.

That is a great thing to say; and which one of us would
not wish that he could say it? "There is that within my soul
which is greater than all circumstances. Whatever happens,
it is not the material fact but the spirit in me that is the
master. Whether I go down to the depths of disappointment
or be lifted up to the heights of my desire, I can keep my
poise unshaken." This is what it would mean to declare,
"I know both how to be abased, and I know how to abound."

James Moffatt in his translation of the New Testament
gives to the familiar words a fresh vividness. He writes them
thus: "I know how to live humbly; I also know how to live
in prosperity." And then come these words following: "I
have been initiated into the secret for all sorts and conditions
of life, for plenty and for hunger, for prosperity and for pri-
vations."

Not in one sermon only, but in two, we shall consider this
great theme.

The period of years beginning about 1930 has been a time
of great and unusual difficulty for multitudes of people. It
has had in it more of privation than of prosperity. There
was an earlier period in America—and that period may return—when our temptations had to do with pride and suc-

[1]From *Great Men of the Bible*, by Walter Russell Bowie, copyrighted 1937 by Harper
& Brothers. Used by permission.

cess. But our recent danger has been that we may feel ourselves beaten down by fears which crush our spirits. In comparison with what we once enjoyed and hoped for, we may seem not to be exalted, but to be abased. But if we are so, the really crucial question still remains to be determined. It is not the fact of being abased, but how to be abased that matters. To know that there are great difficulties may be important; but it is more important to know whether we can meet them greatly.

I

Let us begin by examining those aspects of our life which might make us say in this or any other time that we are abased.

One obvious fact may be that many people may have lost their fortunes. There is a pathos in the poor. There is another and very real pathos in those persons who, having been rich, find themselves reduced to a scale of living which is relatively poor also. They may have been long accustomed both to spend generously and to give generously. They have many people who are dependent upon them—their families, the servants in houses which must be closed, the employees in businesses which must be cut down to skeletons of their former personnel. Material losses may alter the whole surroundings and associations of life. Men must change their occupations and take work which has in it none of the largeness of opportunity which used to be theirs. Women who never had to do so before may have to go out into the business world, with infinite shrinking because of their lack of preparation for it, to earn their livelihood as best they can. They may confess, as they look back on the privileges which formerly they enjoyed, that they lived then in ivory towers; but the towers have tumbled, and they move now on a level whose existence seems to have lost its height and spaciousness. It is unmistakable that their circumstances have been reduced. The danger is that they may begin to think that they, as men and women, also are reduced.

But there is another way in which there may come to many persons the feeling of having been brought down. We look back and see ambitions which have been defeated, or at least so halted that we are not sure that they will ever go forward again. When the year was new, there was some plan on which we had set our hearts. We believed that in the months which then were the future we should carry this through to fine fulfilment; but we have not done it. Always there are those in whose hearts disappointment is echoing like the strokes of an iron bell. Here is a man who launched some venture which he believed would succeed, and it has failed. Here is another who trusted, when the year was young, that the long hard effort to hold some old endangered business together would find at last more favorable auspices; but his hope has been frustrated, and the interests he was trying to safeguard for himself and for many others have gone down to disaster. And here are others, men or women, who in the church or settlement house or other agencies for helping human kind have set in motion eager plans and seen them fail. Such men and women come to the end of their reckoning scarred and wounded. They are like gladiators who have been beaten to their knees by the sword of circumstances which proved too strong for the utmost they could do.

Or again there is a more general way in which it is possible to feel abased—not *de*based, let us always note that the word is, but abased; not dishonored, but brought down from the heights to the flat ground. The influence which accomplishes this for innumerable people is simply the sense that life is passing. They may not have had any particular loss which stands out conspicuously. They may not even have had any specific ambitions set aside. But they are growing more and more acutely conscious of the shortness of time and of the evanescent quality of even their most ambitious efforts. When men and women are young, they feel that there is nothing too large for them to hope to do. The time ahead seems indefinitely long. But as the years go by, the perspective alters. They see how hard it is to point to any accomplishment and how little of what they do accomplish can by any stretch of the imagination be called great. Moreover, the dismaying moment arrives when they perceive that they are no longer the heirs of what once appeared to be an unlimited future. They have come in sight of the time when the span of human life is finished, and when the record of the much or the little which it has accomplished must be made up. Against the background of the past to which already too much of life belongs, and before the future which it will not share, the human spirit is apt to stand with a great sense of loneliness and isolation. The importance which it once took for granted that its career would have seems now to have been only an illusion. Beside the immense and impersonal passage of time, the significance of the one little life seems trivial. It dismays us to reflect how rapidly we have seen each year come and go. Presently in the same fashion years will begin and end which we shall not be here to number. Remembering that, we are prone to think that the utmost we can do is tragically small. It is not that by any particular defeat or disappointment we are abased. It is rather that by our whole consciousness of life's restrictions and relativities we are very much brought low.

II

— Such then are some of the aspects of the reality. When we pass on to consider whether or not they can be met, it is good to remember that we do not have to begin in a vacuum. We can begin with the brave example of a man who met conditions more dispiriting than any we are ever likely to face. The words of the text are like a frame for an heroic face which the centuries have never been able to dim. Paul the Apostle looks at us with his steady eyes as he says: "I know how to be abased." And it is as though he added: "You can know as well."

Let us think, then, of what this man who lived long ago, but whose spirit is greater than any time or place, did experience, and how it was that he prevailed.

First and most obviously, he met the fact of material deprivation. From such fragmentary indications as we can gather, it would seem that Paul had been born into a life of relative abundance. He was not only a Roman citizen; but he had inherited citizenship; that is to say, his father before him was a man of consequence in Cilicia, the province from which he came. He was able to go as a young scholar to the rabbinical school of Gamaliel in Jerusalem, and there he studied for a considerable time. When he became a disciple of Christ, the old ties, of course, were broken. Henceforth, the well-to-do and privileged young scholar became the hated and ostracized representative of a sect which his former associates despised. We hear no more of any ties either with home or former friends. He goes about the world on his far-flung adventure of faith, trusting for the necessities of existence to such work as he himself could do, and to the free-will offerings of the little Christian communities which he formed. We see him in Corinth making tents.

We hear him in his letters referring frequently to gifts which the different Christian congregations had sent him. But sometimes, also, nothing was sent. He knew what it was, he says, to be hungry. Privation was nothing strange to him. But he was not troubled, and above all, he was never bitter. When he wrote Timothy: "Thou therefore endure hardness as a good soldier of Jesus Christ," he was not writing theory, but he was sharing his own high-hearted experience. He was following the Master who had left behind him nothing but the clothes for which Roman legionaries gambled at the foot of the cross. He was following one who had the print of nails in his feet and hands. It did not seem strange to Paul that the *stigmata* of many iron sharpnesses should be in his flesh also. If he were poor, what did that matter? Still he had within him the unsearchable riches of Christ.

Furthermore, he had known the abasement of defeated ambitions. Often we think of Paul through our theological mists. We see him as a finished figure, sometimes almost legendary and non-human, and we do not perceive the poignant human struggles through which he arrived at his final greatness. We see him as a man caught up utterly into the glory of a selfless cause; but we forget the man who must have struggled with an inward agony to crucify all his earlier contrasting hopes. It was no small thing which he had abandoned to be a Christian. He had all the pride of his race and of his class. He had been, as he himself says, "a Pharisee of the Pharisees," born to all the immemorial traditions of Israel. There had been wide open before him the career of a great scholar and teacher, the career most honored and reverenced by those among his own people who had most influenced his thinking. But he had laid all this aside in order to choose something which was more authoritative for his soul. He had felt the overwhelming call to follow and to serve the Christ whose followers once he had persecuted. It was the last thing he had expected. It was in the beginning the last thing he could explain. He only knew that this was the vision his soul must obey. Then as the vision brightened and he went forward in the glory of his new surrender, there were doubtless moments when he saw the possibility of a great triumph for the gospel he was preaching. Perhaps it would kindle like a flame across the world, and innumerable souls would burn like torches to welcome Jesus Christ when he came back to earth again in glory, as Paul at first implicitly believed that he very soon would come. But what happened? The way of preaching and conversion was hard and slow. Here and there souls responded; but there was bitter and malignant opposition among great masses of people in general, and ignorance and human pettiness and much back-sliding even among those who listened to the word. And the glorious day which Paul had hoped for he came presently to understand would never dawn in his time. He had been mistaken in his first conception of an early second advent. The triumph of Christ would not come that way. Through long patience, by infinite faithfulness, and in a vista of time too far for his foreseeing, the Kingdom must be brought about.

So when all was said and done, what was left of his great ambitions? The career he had started on originally had come to its end and to its complete reversal. The second career upon which he had launched had proved very different from what he had expected. It seemed as though there were only a few fragments of his great dream out of which he must lay the foundations of what at best was a future that he should not inherit. And now, as he writes the letter to the

Philippians from which the words of the text are taken, he
is a prisoner in Rome. He is going to die there presently at
the hands of Nero's executioner. It did not seem as though
life which once had aspired to greatness could be more abased
than that.

But the soul of Paul was not abased. There in the deepest
valley he looked upward, and the sunlight of an eternal confidence was in his eyes. What did it matter that his first ambitions were set at naught? He would consider simply that the
architecture of his mind had been too small. He would take
the broken stones of his old imaginations and build them into
the outlines of a mightier hope which God would bring to
pass. If his ambitions had been defeated, it was only that
God's infinite aims for him might be set free.

And, in the third place, Paul must have felt that general
depression which accompanies the mood of every dying year.
Paul was thinking, not only of the dying year, but of the
dying moments of life itself. His time was short, and he knew
it. How little of all that he had wanted to do had yet been
done! How inadequate life seemed, and how short its horizon as compared with its range of hopes! It was not only
that he himself seemed frustrated as an individual. Often he
must have had dark moments of brooding as to whether
humanity itself might not be frustrated in the conflict of its
aspirations with all the heavy evil of the world. Was this all
it meant for Christ to have died on the cross: that he himself, Christ's follower, must also die in the midst of a world
that seemed as pagan as it had ever been? In thoughts like
these, there was the possibility that his soul might have been
brought altogether to humiliation. But here also he knew
how to be abased. He had already learned how to conquer
deprivation and disappointment. He could arm himself

now at the last against despair. Past all the resources of his
own life or the life of his generation, he relied upon the infinite reserves of God. "In all these things," he could cry,
"we are more than conquerors through him that loved us."
He trusted in Him with whom a day is as a thousand years
and a thousand years as one day.

III

We have considered the facts by which lives in our time
and in all times may be abased. We have considered one
great figure who met his abasement in such fashion that the
greatness of his soul was the more revealed. We pass on
finally to consider the meaning of his secret as it applies to us.

Take first the fact of the loss of material things. It is
possible, of course, for that to seem only a disaster. It may
be like the crumbling of the structure which a man has
laboriously built around and above himself, so that he himself is crushed and buried in its ruins. But if they are
grandly treated, the same facts can present an altogether
different picture. They can be the taking away of the
ornate draperies which have been wrapped around a man,
so that for the first time the nobility of his own simple and
unadorned self may be revealed.

The only tragedy in loss of fortune, and even in great
deprivation, is among those who show that they have not
now, and perhaps have never had, any high belief in their
own selves. They have thought they were important as long
as they had an important place in the world of society, or
could move with the freedom which much money gives.
Now that suddenly they have become poor, or almost poor,
they are sensitive to the point of mental agony. They feel
as people feel sometimes in those strange nightmares when

they dream that they are naked in the midst of a staring and deriding crowd. So men and women stripped of their wealth may feel embarrassed and humiliated. They want to hide the fact of it; and if they cannot hide that, they shrink away and hide themselves furtively from their former associations.

But what is there in poverty, either relative or absolute, to bring defeat upon any man or woman so long as the soul within is brave and true? Francis of Assisi, one of the most joyous and radiant figures that ever trod this earth, was known as "the little poor man of Assisi." Martin Luther, who shook a continent with his moral power, was born poor, and remained so all his life, and he gloried in it. "Poor men's sons," he said, "must labor to lift themselves out of the dust, and must endure greatly; and because they have nothing to boast about or pride themselves upon, they trust God, control themselves, and keep still." Paul the Apostle was poor; and yet he went about all his gallant business with a song. Jesus Christ was poor; and he could say of himself, with no hint of self-pity but with heroic freedom, "The foxes have holes, and the birds of the air have nests; but the Son of Man hath not where to lay his head." Why then should the mere loss of money dismay a man or make any man think that his life need for that fact have any less significance? God give us all, to begin with, a brave truthfulness! If any man has lost money, yes, if materially he has lost everything, let him not try to conceal it and torture himself either with pretense or with evasion. Let him be ready that everybody with whom he has had associations should know the facts simply and naturally, and without either apology or parade; and let him be sure that in the moment when he realizes that there is no longer any possibility of any one valuing him merely for what he has, then for the first time there may arise, both among his friends and within himself, a clear and virile new conception of what he *is*.

Have we not seen the reality of this all round us in these days? Every one of us can name friends who have endured loss of fortune and met that loss with a courage and constancy which has made them seem far bigger and more admirable people than we knew they were before. There are men who have had to give up great positions of leadership and abandon the benefactions which once they rejoiced in. A mean spirit put in that position would imagine that it could no longer live happily as it used to do before. But the big man shows within himself the kind of unabashed sincerity which burns like a flame that needs nothing beyond itself to make it into light and power. There are men today who, because of their own loss of opportunity, have come into inspiring new fellowship with other men. They have made those who used to be upon a lesser level of position, and were envious of what they thought was the great man's accidental greatness of opportunity, be envious no more. In place of envy, there is admiration, and a desire to learn what it is that can make the one who seemed a big man when he was exalted seem an even bigger man now, when, by the measurements of the world, he is abased. They love him for his self-reliance, his uncomplaining courage, and his steady willingness to give himself, and not to think that this self-giving is of any less worth now that he has no material things to give with it. And there are women too whose examples have had the same effect. Some of them have through all their lives been in positions of privilege. They have never done any hard work, even in their own households. But circumstances have changed now, and they have shown themselves surprisingly equipped to meet them. They have undertaken labors which they never would have thought they could accomplish, and in so doing they have revealed a humour, a good temper, and a cheerfulness which have given to their families and to their friends something that no money could ever conceivably have bought. Why then should any living persons today be unduly frightened lest materially they should be abased? It is possible to learn how to be abased, and out of abasement to rise with a grander and more evident integrity of soul—as the chiseled statue rises to its serene proportions the more the concealing marble is cut away.

But what shall we do when our abasement comes through some defeated ambition and frustrated aim?

Well, we may rightly approach our answer here by considering what we must *not* do. We must not begin by blaming circumstances. It is possible that circumstances may be to blame, but we can discover that later. The first thing we want is an honest consideration of what measure of blame there may be in us.

That was what Paul always did. He did not sit down and lay his difficulties at the door of fate. He inquired first what there was in himself to be set right. He examined his own soul to see if there was any evil in him, and often he found that there was. He said that there was a law in his members warring against the law of his mind. There was that in his flesh which struggled against the spirit. He did not spare these evils which he saw in his own nature. He did not try to rationalize them nor to deal with them by excuses and evasion. He confronted them with honesty and called upon every resource in his own soul, and cried out in

his prayer upon all the resources of God, to help him overcome them. He disciplined himself, that all his appetites
should be made subject to his aspirations. "So fight I, not
as one that beateth the air," he said. "But I keep under my
body, and bring it into subjection: lest that by any means,
when I have preached to others, I myself should be a cast-
away." He knew that he had no right to blame circumstances until he had done his best to see that his own soul
was girded for effective action.

Surely there are many of us who can recognize the bearing
of that upon our own realities. We look back and see the
things in which we have more or less completely failed. Some
of them may have been good and great aims in which we
think that we ought to have succeeded. The world would
have seemed better, and the universe a place where it would
have been easier to believe in the providence of God, if we
had achieved those ends which appeared to be endued with
the highest values that we knew. But we did not achieve
them. And then what? Shall we stand and whimper before the face of fate? Shall we salve our vanity by saying
that failure was due to the force of circumstances? Or shall
we not better begin by being rigorous with ourselves? What
flaws in our mental or moral forces may have been at least
in part responsible? Where have we been secretly indolent
even when we have appeared to be industrious; where have
we dodged the difficult and important matters in order to be
busy about secondary and more agreeable ones; where have
we failed in the self-discipline which would have made us do
the things which needed to be done, but which we pretended
we were not equipped for and left to the chance that some
one else would do them? These are the questions we need
to answer, and upon the results of which we need to act. It

may be too late to save the particular ambition or to carry
through the particular plan on which we once adventured.
But it is not too late to save the possibilities of ourselves for
larger and better enterprise tomorrow. Some of life's greatest blessings come out of temporary defeat. One man by his
reverses may be soured and halted; another will be corrected,
made more clear in his perceptions, and more resolute in his
will. The only real failures are among those who treat the
obstacle as though it were the end of the road. When we
find an obstacle, or when through our fault we know that we
have created it, the thing to do is to set to work at the personal self-discipline which can make us able to surmount
that obstacle and whatever others may lie beyond. There is
one word which every single one should bar out of his or her
vocabulary for ever, and that word is *discouraging*. A thing
may be disturbing, yes; it may be disappointing, yes; but
discouraging, no! No man ever can be abased as long as
his courage burns; and no outward facts can quench his
inner courage if to the flame of it he brings the fuel of his
patience, his perseverance, and his prayer.

But what if it be true that after a man has examined himself and corrected himself, still beyond the utmost which he
can accomplish, the fact remains that his high desires are
blocked and his plans defeated? Then let him put the issue up
to God, and go on. It may be that some time tomorrow the
gates in the iron wall which seems to hedge him round will
suddenly open, and all his joyous desires will go forward into
the spacious freedom he has longed for. But it may be that
the gates through which he longed to go will remain barred,
not because God does not mean him to go forward, but
because He means him to go forward in another way. That
happened more than once in the great career of Paul.

Things which seemed at the moment to be the disintegration of his hopes were only the pressure of God's hands, withholding him from the smaller satisfaction, that he might be turned to the mightier purpose which otherwise he would not have seen.   And in many of the experiences of our own time that same reality is evident.   Surely there are few men and women who, looking back thoughtfully upon their own lives, can fail to know that many of the things which at the moment seemed cruel disappointments were, as one has put it, *His appointments.*   Past their own blocked roadways, God has opened ascending paths to hilltops of accomplishment which else they never would have scaled.

Finally, we come again to that sort of abasement which is most sure at last to fall upon us, and ask ourselves how we shall deal also with that.   When life seems short, and the years go fast, and our personal accomplishment seems so limited, how shall we still believe in the glory of life?

The way of the answer must lie through a transfer of our consideration from ourselves to that which is greater than ourselves.   Paul was not concerned about his own record or about what his life amounted to, because his thought was merged in a loyalty which embraced in its great certainty all these lesser questionings.   He had identified himself with the Kingdom of God as it was made beautiful to him in the spirit of his Master.   He wrote for other men what he had proven true for himself: "Whether we live therefore, or die, we are the Lord's."   He did not measure time by the span of his own existence.   He did not measure results by what happened to him or through him.   He was a part of something infinitely more grand, which gave stability and meaning to everything he might be or do, and which extended all the perspective of his hope.   No matter how his present fortunes might seem to be abased, the real Paul could never be abased, because in his thought, in his love, and in his dedication, he was made one with the will of God.

What that means we have seen in many nearer instances. The beauty of the lives of the noblest women finds its interpretation here. The mother identifies herself with her husband, her children, and her home. She does not henceforth think of herself in a narrow and isolated way; and whether for the moment she gains what she might have desired does not greatly matter. The thing she lives for is the life of the larger group she loves. As long as that is being advanced, and she knows it is advanced in a thousand secret ways which the world can never measure, nothing which happens to her can ever quench her gladness. She will stoop to the royalty of the lowliest service in that same spirit with which Jesus on the last night in the upper room girded himself with a towel and washed the disciples' feet.

There are other figures also out in the wider life of human kind who have learned this identification of themselves with great loyalties which neither time nor fortune can affect. As Disraeli said of Richard Cobden when that great member of Parliament and leader of the public life of England died, "There are those who are independent of dissolutions, of the caprices of constituencies, and even of the course of time." Remember that whenever life's prospects seem to wane. There is forever a greatness of soul and a greatness of service which are independent of the course of time. The secret is in the immortal words of that great soul who has already furnished so much of the material of our thinking now. "I live," said Paul, "yet not I, but Christ liveth in me." All narrowness of personal self-seeking, all pettiness of concern for personal fortune and for personal praise, had been lifted upward and turned to brighter flame in the fire of his devotion to the purposes of God as these were revealed to him in Christ. When that had happened, nothing in him could really be a failure. All there was of him that was petty would fall away like ashes drifting to the ground. But all in him that was immortal would blend in joyous splendor with the blaze of the glory of God. Thus, and thus only, was he abased; and out of that abasement, he knew, and he can make us know, what it was triumphantly to abound.

VIII

Jack Finegan:
Helping Students Face
The Issues of Life

John R. Mott once said that if he had his life to live over again he would place himself alongside a great university, for some of the greatest needs and opportunities of our day are there. He felt that students were "strategically the most important people in the world." They are still in the formative stages of life. They are in the top ten per cent of the population in terms of intellectual ability. They will provide the leadership of tomorrow. They also have problems. They are faced with life's permanent choices: the choice of a life vocation, the choice of a life partner, and the choice of a life philosophy. They are determining the ultimate aims, goals, and loyalties by which they will live. Sometimes this is not easy. They are forced to think through the implications of science, philosophy, psychology, history, and all of the rest of modern learning as it relates to religious faith and the Christian life. Many are away from home for the first time. The moral restraints of family, church, and community are gone. Some have financial worries, some moral questions, some are having difficulty in their academic program, some are lonely and homesick, some become discouraged. The average student is involved in a multitude of activities that consume his time and energy. All this results in some tension and, at times, much uncertainty.

151

Chad Walsh describes the modern student in these terms: "He is confused, well-meaning, likeable, quietly wistful for something—he isn't quite sure what."[1] This is not fair to some students, for many are sincere and well-adjusted, but they all have their problems and their needs. To help young people face these issues of life is a great responsibility. It will be done not by preaching alone, but by personal counseling, by the activities of student groups, by the guidance of professors and specialists in various fields that are present on our modern campuses—but preaching too has a vital part in the total picture. If preaching is done well, it can do much to help young people grow in their faith as they grow in their professional and academic training. It can help them face their personal problems and discouragements and challenge them with high ideals of character and service. Anyone who serves a church which includes students faces a great challenge.

Dr. Jack Finegan has spent most of his life in a university atmosphere and in contact with students. He holds five graduate degrees including the doctoral degree of Lic. theol. *magna cum laude* from the University of Berlin. He has served as the pastor of a church adjoining a campus, a director of religious life on a state university campus, a professor of religion both at the undergraduate and graduate level. At the present time he is a professor at the Pacific School of Religion and is the pastor of the University Christian Church, Berkeley, California.

His writings in the field of archeology and the Bible have established him as a scholar in his own right. However, his concerns for scholarship have not separated him from the personal and religious problems of students. Parallel with

---

[1]Walsh: "Flat Minds, Kind Hearts, and Fine Arts," from *The Christian Scholar,* Vol. XXXVI, No. 2, June 1953, p. 100.

his writings in these more technical fields has been a series of publications prepared to meet the needs of students. These include books of sermons to youth entitled *A Highway Shall Be There* (Bethany Press 1916), and *Like the Great Mountains* (Bethany Press 1949), a book of *Student Prayers* (Association Press 1946), and a book entitled *Youth Asks About Religion* (Association Press 1949). This latter volume grew out of his personal contacts with students. It consists of one hundred questions which young people face. "The questions," he said, "are such as I have often been asked in classrooms, church, and home, in conference and convention, in groups and by individuals." In speaking of his manner of facing such questions, he said, "I have never tried to give a final pronouncement, but only reply frankly and honestly, in the light of my present state of knowledge and faith, to frank and honest inquiries."

Such honest dealing with real issues, whether in the private interview or from the pulpit, can do much to aid students in these significant years in their lives. When he speaks to students he speaks very simply and very clearly, as in this sermon, "Thank God and Take Courage!"

THANK GOD AND TAKE COURAGE![1]

By Jack Finegan

What the average man has to thank God for includes his life itself. The ordinary person is endowed with a good body and mind. He is the master of a marvelous human machine which, with all due respect to the fine machines of the modern world, is more wonderful still. Even on the organic side alone, as Professor J. A. Thompson remarks, it is a "self-stoking, self-repairing, self-preserving, self-adjusting, self-increasing, self-reproducing engine"—all of which are quite unusual qualities for a "machine." On the mental and spiritual sides the human person has faculties which utterly transcend anything observable anywhere else in the universe.

This we all have, and this none of us has created for himself. My existence is my most immediately certain fact, yet this is the thing I have done least of all to create. We had little to do with the fact that among millions of galaxies and billions of suns, there is a habitable home here on earth, a home, as G. W. Gray puts it, between two fires, "the banked embers of the cooling star fragment on which we live, and the flaming incandescence of the star we are hitched to." Among the millions of combinations mathematically possible, as Professor L. J. Henderson points out, there actually occurred on this earth and in its atmosphere the very elements—oxygen, hydrogen, and carbon, and their compounds, water and carbonic acid—best fitted to favor the appearance of life. Likewise, the continuance of life is due largely to great sustaining forces, which we do not create but at best only learn somewhat to cooperate with. Dr. R. C. Cabot remarks that every dirty splinter we get into our hands might be fatal, were it not for the dramatic fight put up for us by the little creatures called leucocytes, or white corpuscles, which hasten to the spot and, dying in the fight, pile up their bodies to make a wall of defense between the attacking bacteria and the free circulation. Countless other such illustrations of defense, compensation, balance, and reserve with the human body are ascribable to the *vis medicatrix naturae,* "the healing power of nature," which Cabot and Dicks prefer to call the *vis medicatrix Dei,* "the healing power of God."

For all of this we are dependent, not upon ourselves, nor hardly upon blind and mechanical forces, but rather upon the teleological, end-seeking purposes of God. We thank God for it, and if we do, then we seek to keep this life most highly attuned for the tasks of which it is capable. My friend is an aviator, and I have stood on a verdant Hawaiian island and watched him fling his plane aloft, where one must fly almost constantly on a sharp bank to stay over the diminutive island, elsewhere being only the endless Pacific. But he never flew until the best mechanics had tested the motor, the struts, and every square foot of the gleaming plane, and he himself had listened with practiced ear to the drone of the engine and given swift and accurate inspection to all the instruments upon which his life, in a moment, would depend. He flew with no dizzy compass, no coughing, wheezing motor, no sluggish controls, but with a plane in tune. If we thank God for body, mind, and soul, then we pray, too, that we may keep them in tune for the high flights of which they are capable.

The average man also has a great world for which to thank God. Early one morning I stood on the summit of Longs Peak, at an elevation of 14,255 feet, while the sun etched sharply a superb spectacle. The north face, up which we had come, dropped off to the Boulder Field, whose granite masses seemed but pebbles, the east precipice fell 2,400 feet to Chasm Lake, while on the west the cliffs sloped precipitously 3,000 feet down into Glacier Gorge. Splintered crags adorned a ridge which projected itself like a flying buttress against the lower side of the mountain. Snow fields hung on canyon walls and ended in cold, green lakes. Range after range of snow-capped mountains marched away to the horizon. What a terrific and awesome world it was, fit dwelling of the Spirit of God, and yet it is our world, too. We may climb its peaks and cross its seas, explore its atoms and, by the magic of light and thought, traverse its galaxies. We rejoice that it is vast, varied, and amazing, dependable, orderly, and meaningful. We thank God for this, which the Greeks called the *cosmos,* the orderly universe, and also for what they called the *oecumene,* the inhabited world, old enough to be rich, and young enough to be pliant. The average man has all of this and needs only to open his eyes to it to be moved to thank God for it.

The ordinary person also has at least some people for whom to be thankful. Among these, for most of us, are our families. Slightly to paraphrase Sir Walter Scott:

> Breathes there the man with soul so dead
> Who never to himself hath said:
>   "This is my own, my own dear home"?
> Whose heart hath ne'er within him burned
> As home his footsteps he hath turned
>   From lands where he was wont to roam?
> If such there breathe, go mark him well;
> For him no minstrel raptures swell;

High though his titles, proud his name,
Boundless his wealth as wish can claim,
Despite those titles, power and pelf,
The wretch concentrated all in self,
Living, shall forfeit fair renown,
And, doubly dying, shall go down
To the vile dust from whence he sprung,
Unwept, unhonored, and unsung.

Most of us have friends, too, sweethearts and companions, and for all those who understand us, share life with us, look into our eyes and clasp our hands, we thank God!

It is true that among people we find our greatest troubles. A familiar hymn sings of a tropical isle, where "every prospect pleases, and only man is vile." Tennyson spoke of "Nature, red in tooth and claw," but man's battlefields outdo the savagery of the jungle. Dr. Hans Zinsser of Harvard remarks that there are only two kinds of living things which make ferocious war upon their own kind—rats and men.

But among men also are the greatest possibilities for good. Man not only practices war, but also dreams of peace; not only manufactures bombs, but also strives to build a society of nations. Among men exists the ideal of overcoming strife by brotherhood, hate by love, and evil by good. Among families and friends we see already at work the great principles which can build a happier world, Christianity's respect for the value of personality, the Golden Rule's mutual concern, the Cross's sacrificial love. If, then, I thank God for people, let me, myself, "live in a house by the side of the road . . . and be a friend to man."

If we thank God for life, the world, and people, we cannot but be haunted by the remembrance that while we have health, others have sickness; while our sky is bright, the sky is dark above others with strife; while we enjoy friends and dear ones, others are homeless and outcast and have no opportunity for friends save in slums or adjoining prison cells. Whereupon, we thank God for one man's chance to make things better. For the average man has this, too. Basil King and Channing Pollock were sitting together in a restaurant when a woman at an adjoining table said to her companion, "It's a disgraceful state of affairs, but what can one man do?" The author of *The Conquest of Fear* looked at the man who wrote *The Fool* and asked, "Shall we tell her that everything of importance in the world was begun by one man—or one woman?" Under the title *One Man Power,* Channing Pollock went on to describe the abolition of slums, the reform of prisons, the beginning of the American Red Cross, the origin of the Braille system, the rise of Tuskegee Institute, and many another such thing, pointing out that again and again it has been a single man or woman who has raised a banner lone-handed, behind which eventually thousands have enlisted.

It is the kind of world where one man can make a difference, where the very stars in their courses fight with heroes and crusaders. Professor Harry A. Overstreet even defines religion as "the kind of belief in the universe that quickens me in all my upgoing trends." We thank God for this. We thank God for the One and his leadership. He was but one lone person, wearing the name of the Christ, living one solitary life, yet, as Jean Paul Richter said, he "lifted with pierced hand empires off their hinges, and turned the stream of centuries out of its channel, and still governs the ages."

Finally, we thank God for the triumph that is possible over trial and tribulation. The ordinary person certainly experiences trouble. We do not thank God for trouble itself, for we believe that his heart is broken, too, by evil and that he shares the pain of men. But we thank him for the triumph that is possible.

Demosthenes stuttered, Steinmetz was dwarfed and deformed, Milton was blind, and Francis Thompson tubercu-
lar. Robert Louis Stevenson was sick most of his life, yet
the worst years from the standpoint of suffering were the
most productive in literary work. Pasteur made his most
valuable discovery after a stroke of apoplexy. After Beethoven grew completely deaf, his work attained sublimity.

At Harvard one evening, a freshman named William Prescott walked into a room where some of his classmates were
still enjoying themselves after dinner. One hurled a heavy
crust of bread across the room just as Prescott entered. He
was struck squarely in the eyes, and fell to the floor. The
best oculists in Boston could save only a dim part of the
sight of one eye. He completed his course as best he could,
then tried work and travel in turn, but found that the eye
grew worse rather than better. Five years after he had entered college dreaming of greatness, his only exercise was to
walk by the hour, with outstretched arms, in a room so dark
that not even the furniture was visible. But suddenly, in
1820, William Prescott announced that he intended to become a historian. In a darkened study Prescott sat for six
hours every day, listening and memorizing, while assistants
read to him from reference books. Then he dictated, paragraph by paragraph, and when his first volume was finished,
it told the story of Spain during the reign of Ferdinand and
Isabella. The second described the Spanish conquest of
Mexico; the third narrated the history of Peru. When he
died after thirty-nine years of work, he had written sixteen
thick volumes of such character as to bring him world-wide
fame.

Thank God and take courage! It was probably in the
early spring of the year 60, on the famous Appian Way, a
few miles outside Rome, that a prisoner was moving wearily

along in the custody of a Roman centurion. A long and hazardous winter voyage, involving shipwreck, was behind him; ahead was imprisonment, trial, and ultimately a martyr death under Nero. The prisoner's name was Paul, and there at the Market of Appius and the Three Taverns he was met by Christian brethren who had come out to greet him. For the blessing of this refreshing meeting, but still with shipwreck behind and uncertainty before, Paul "thanked God and took courage." (Acts 25:15.)[1] Sometime within the next two years, from a rude dwelling where he was chained to a Roman soldier, Paul wrote this in a letter:

> I have learned how to be content wherever I am. . . .
> I have been initiated into the secret for all sorts and conditions of life, for plenty and for hunger, for prosperity and for privations. In him who strengthens me I am able for anything. (Phil. 4: 11-12.)[1]

In the name of him who strengthened Paul, thank God and take courage!

---

[1]From *The Bible: A New Translation*, by James Moffatt. Copyrighted 1922, 1935 and 1950 by Harper & Brothers. Used by permission.

IX

Ralph W. Sockman:
With Older People
In Mind

When we began collecting this series of sermons, it was
felt that there should be at least one sermon that dealt with
the problems of older people. Such sermons are not easy to
find. There are many sermons on the problems of youth,
not many on the problems of older people. There are some
exceptions, like Dr. Fosdick's *Temptations of Maturity,* but
they are rather rare. It has been the subject of innumerable
articles, addresses, even of books, but not of sermons. Medical, sociological, and psychological circles have been giving
increasing attention to the field of geriatrics. It is recognized
as one of the sociological phenomena of our day. Since the
turn of the century the average life expectancy has increased
from fifteen to twenty years. There are more older people in
society than in any previous generation. Since 1940 the
number of people in America sixty years of age and older has
increased by 33 per cent. One out of every ten persons in
the average community is above what government and in-
dustry consider retirement age. All surveys emphasize that
this trend will increase. These people are in our churches.
They will be there in increasing proportion. It has been said
that science has added years to our lives. It is the task of
the church to add life to our years.

This sermon by Dr. Sockman on "A Truce with Time" deals with this issue. All of his ministry has been in one church, the Christ Methodist Church in New York City. Through his radio preaching and his numerous books he has extended his influence far beyond his local parish.

The selection of a sermon on the needs of older people does not mean to imply that this is the only, or even the major, emphasis of his preaching. Anyone familiar with his books knows that he discusses a wide variety of both personal and social issues. He is basically what might be termed a "life-situation preacher." When he gave the Lyman Beecher lectures on preaching, he stated the principles and philosophy behind his own pulpit work. Some quotations from these lectures are worthy of note. "The preacher," he said, "will prepare his sermons with the needs of his people in mind. He will visualize individuals whose secret cares have been revealed to him. His messages will grow out of life situations. He will preach to problems yet not as problems." . . . "Starting where people live, he will be sure of their interest at the very beginning; but he thereby assumes a high responsibility, for unless he arrives somewhere he will be equally sure of the listeners' disappointment, if not disgust at the end. Preaching to life situations is the most fruitful form of sermonizing but it requires the deepest roots. The one who does it must have the people not only in his mind but on his heart."

He recognized that such preaching had certain dangers and must be rooted in the heritage of the Christian faith.

> In order to prevent an introspective self-centeredness and preserve the full orb of the Christian message, life-situation preaching should be blended with Biblical exposition and doctrinal teaching. . . . When we start with life situations we start where

men live, then lead the questioning soul to the doctrinal and Biblical sources. . . . The sermon will ar-
rest the attention of the hearer with a real issue and
then direct the quest to the ever-satisfying Scriptures.
It is the project method applied to the Bible. Such
preaching will combine the teaching quality with
the intensely practical. Yet, instead of reducing
the "power from on high" to the scale of our petty
concerns, it leads us to the "secret place of the Most
High" where we abide "under the shadow of the
Almighty."[1]

The way he applied such principles can be seen in the sermon
that follows.

---

[1]From *The Highway of God.* Used by permission of Ralph W. Sockman.

A TRUCE WITH TIME[1]

By Ralph W. Sockman

Shortly after the United States entered the Great War,
Lord Balfour of England and Henri Bergson, the distinguished philosopher of France, were together in New York
City. They had come to arouse American interest in the
cause of the Allies. After speaking at a great mass meeting
they retired to the home of Joseph H. Choate. There, while
the city was seething with war excitement, these two eminent
representatives of their respective governments talked long
into the night. About what? The military crisis? No.
They discussed the immortality of the soul.

In the midst of the most immediate problems, there are
certain timeless questions which are always timely. Our attitude toward these eternal issues serves to steady or weaken
our morale in facing current concerns. And for a proper
relationship to contemporary affairs, perhaps nothing is more
basic than a right adjustment to time itself.

The element of time is a very present one to most persons.
Every modern contrivance seems conspiring to make us conscious of time. We live and move and have our being in the
presence of clocks. The progressive shift of population from
the soil to the city has transferred us from the timing of the
seasons to the staccato of train schedules and ticker-tapes.
And the spread of urban conditions to the country has
brought the wages-and-hours calculations to the farm. If

[1]From *Live for Tomorrow*, by Ralph W. Sockman, copyright 1942, The Macmillan
Company. Used by permission.

we so enjoy our work that we never watch the clock, sooner or later we do look at the calendar. Even though buoyant health may make us smile at the passing years, competitive business all too soon reminds us that age does count. Children talk much about their birthdays, yet worry little about them. Their elders talk little about their age, yet worry much about it.

And having become time-conscious, most of us think of time as an enemy. We call him Father Time, but we picture him as a grim reaper with a scythe. This should not be so to those who have learned the mastery of life from the Great Teacher. The good life declares a truce with time, even transforming the enemy into an ally.

The first simple suggestion for this truce is to stop fighting time as if it were the foe of our usefulness. The desire to be of use is a major factor in making life worth living. The deepest need of our natures is to feel that we are needed. And to be sure, time does seem to put a terminus both to our marketable work and often to those personal responsibilities which make us feel that we are playing a vital part in the family or social group. In fact, our high-powered machine culture appears to make ever shorter the period of a man's productive years. Any person over forty knows the tragic realities of the dead-line set by age in the industrial world. One of the dilemmas of our day is that while our medical science is prolonging our years of possible activity, our economic science seems unable to find occupations for the years we are lengthening. Certainly the plainest of Christian duties is to do all in our power as a society to make old age secure.

But mere economic security is no satisfying answer to man's craving for life. It does not fulfill the wish to be of use. We are born with creative desires, and the strategy of living is to keep these functioning to the farthest reach of our years. These must therefore find scope in realms outside the office and factory, and then when age brings us to what is called retirement, we do not topple over like spinning tops which have run down. We can be kept going by finding a usefulness beyond the measure of the public market place.

When we leave the realm of commercial rewards and enter the sphere of values, there is no competition to crowd us out. There is no law of supply and demand to limit the production of beauty, truth, and goodness. One of the heartening phases of modern life is the new usefulness being discovered by middle-aged mothers after their child-rearing duties are done. Their activities are expanding into the realms of public service, adult education, the fine arts; and their earlier labors, which were assumed to leave our grand-mothers exhausted and ready for the fireside nooks, are now being revealed as the means of enrichment for further service. Do not the experiences of motherhood sharpen the artistic insight and do not long years of human contact deepen the understanding essential to effective writing? Why should not tomorrow blossom with budding autumnal artists and writers to supplement the current vogue of youthfulness?

There is good precedent for predicting an extension of usefulness beyond the "dead-line" of age. Immanuel Kant was seventy-four when he wrote his "Metaphysics of Ethics." Tintoretto was the same age when he painted his vast canvas of "Paradiso." John Wesley, when past eighty, was still preaching up and down England saying with a smile, "'Tis time to live if I grow old."

> Is it too late? Ah, nothing is too late
> Till the tired heart shall cease to palpitate.
> Cato learned Greek at eighty; Sophocles
> Wrote his grand "Oedipus" and Simonides
> Bore off the prize of verse from his compeers
> When each had numbered more than four score years.

. . .
Chaucer at Woodstock with the nightingales
At sixty wrote the "Canterbury Tales."
Goethe at Weimar, toiling to the last,
Completed "Faust" when cighty years were past.
These are indeed exceptions; but they show
How far the Gulf Stream of our youth may flow
Into the Arctic regions of our lives,
Where little else than life itself survives.[2]

In answer to such a list it may be said that the citations
of genius do not help the situations of the commonplace.
Granted that not many of us can use our later years to produce noteworthy creations of pen or canvas, usefulness is
not confined to such spectacular contributions. In mind at
the moment is an unmarried aunt no longer able to find
commercial employment and not capable of creating artistic
things. Yet by her spirit of cheerful fortitude and contagious
coöperation, she is worth immeasurably much to both the
younger and older members of the household. And do not
most of us know some elderly persons who stand serenely
above the heat and tension of surface living, their white
heads rendering to the circles around them a service comparable to the lift given by a snowclad peak to a traveler in
the lowlands? They catch the first tints of the dawn and
hold the lingering rays of the setting sun. These wise and
godly elders anticipate the hopes of youth and lengthen the
days of the adults. And from their summits of experience
they catch the intimations of that larger life which "eye
hath not seen, nor ear heard."[3] Yes, "They also serve who
only stand and wait."

A second suggestion for a truce with time is to cease fighting age as if it were the foe of our pleasures. We take it for

[2]Longfellow, Henry W., "Morituri Salutamus."
[3]1 Corinthians 2: 9.

granted that we "must go it while we are young" and that, as Ecclesiastes put it, "the years draw nigh, when thou shalt say, I have no pleasure in them."[4]   Admittedly youth has a tremendous capacity for pleasure.   The young in their exuberance of energy rush from excitement to excitement. And in time such vitality does abate.   But life has its seasonal compensations, and those who learn its rhythm find it no anticlimax to move from flaming youth to the thrifty, home-building thirties, the roaring forties, the full fifties and the serene sixties.

One of the compensations of time is that when it takes away youth it leaves memories which are even more pleasant than those early experiences were at the time.   Thomas Carlyle once parried the question as to why the past looks so beautiful to us.   In answer he suggested this reason: "It is because fear has been extracted from it, for one thing." We see his point.   When a pleasure is in prospect, we are disturbed by the fear that it may not be realized, but a pleasure in retrospect is secure.   When we look back on the days of our youth, we tend to think of them as almost unalloyed delight.   But they were not.   They were filled with fears.   Perhaps mine was a nature unduly disposed to worry, but I was wont to becloud the approach to a vacation or excursion by counting impatiently the days remaining until the big event.   And then when I was on my vacation or excursion, I proceeded to count gloomily the dwindling number of days left to be enjoyed.   Thus I tended to overshadow both the beginning and the end of many a good time.   But now in my memory I dwell on those pleasant occasions without the accompanying shadows.

---

[4] Ecclesiastes 12: 1.

Yet the custodianship of memory is not an adequate preservative of pleasure. Too tame is it merely to contemplate our good times in retrospect. We must get a grip on our high moments which is not loosened by the passage of time. It would seem that our enthusiasms grow more short-lived as the tempo of living is speeded up. Whittier's barefoot boy seemed to get a longer enjoyment from his simple homemade playthings than does the modern lad from his elaborate amusement devices and ever-changing movies. And we adults are prone to neglect the lasting things in our search for the latest things. Sensations chase one another across the front pages of our papers, and no single event is spectacular enough to hold the public interest for more than a few days. In trying to keep up to the minute, our interests tend to become momentary.

Vicki Baum in "Grand Hotel" graphically describes this elusiveness: "The real thing is always going on somewhere else. When you are young, you think it will come later. Later on, you think it was earlier. When you are here, you think it is there. But when you get there, you find that life has doubled back and is quietly waiting here, here in the very place you ran away from. It is the same with life as it is with the butterfly collector and the swallow tail. As you see it flying away it is wonderful. But as soon as it is caught, the colors are gone and the wings bashed."

The good life partakes of that spirit of sport which throws itself wholeheartedly into every game as if that were the sole object in life and yet is not undone by success or failure when the particular game is over. And how are we able to put ourselves wholly into the pleasures of the present and then to keep our hearts whole when those experiences are passed? By realizing that the sources of satisfaction are carried within our own spirits rather than in the things to be enjoyed. The relation of a joyous experience to a person is like that of the weight of a book to the earth. Where does the weight of the book reside? Well, we could change its weight without tearing a leaf from its pages if we could alter its relation to the earth. It is the force of the earth's gravity which helps to determine the weight of a book. It is the health of the eater which helps to make the food seem good. Obvious, even trite, as this truth is, most of us have not lived our way into it. We have not learned to transfer our treasures of pleasure from the external realm "where moth and rust doth corrupt and where thieves break through and steal." We have not appropriated the truth of the Kingdom of Heaven within us and thus beyond the reach of time's wear and tear.

When we have really learned this secret of the good life, we "have builded a house which is not for time's throwing." Time may have taken away the money which we had ten years ago; time removes from us the sports in which we were once able to indulge; age deprives us eventually of the travel we once relished. But when we take to heart the truth that "though the outer man perish, yet the inner man is renewed day by day," then time instead of impoverishing us enriches by capitalizing our past experiences. As our inner capital grows, our interest in the present increases. We are able to make more out of simple things. Well-ripened age gets far more joy out of a June day or an evening's conversation than does raw youth.

When I take a trip with my seventeen-year-old daughter, I enjoy the experience with more tenses than does she, for I have the present sensations provided by the sights we see, plus the memory of my own youthful trips with my father, plus the added insight which my wider travels have given me, plus the vicarious enjoyment which a parent gets from the pleasures of his child. Thus the added tenses of age more than match the intensity of youth.

Anatole France, in "The Garden of Epicurus," whimsically remarked that had he been given the privilege of creating man, he would have done so on the pattern not of the biped, but of the caterpillar, for the former starts life upright and then verges toward the earth, while the latter starts life horizontally but later wings its way upward. Physically, to be sure, we are bipeds, but spiritually we can live on an ascending scale.

And now a third suggestion for this truce with time. We should cease fighting time as the foe of our affections. So many of our books, motion pictures and common observations give the impression that love grows stodgy and tarnished with age.

The native passions do lose their ardor. The physical fuel which sustains "the flame of youth" is not inexhaustible. But the light which feeds from its own candle can with the passing years be changed into an incandescence whose radiance comes from a larger source. Yonder is an acquaintance now past eighty. Instead of the years causing a dimming of the lights, his is a case of lights coming on at eventide. He is alive at more points today than sixty years ago. The doctors have kept his body alive, but the Great Physician has kept his spirit alive—alive to the needs of others, alive to the bubbling joys of little children, alive to the appeal of art, alive to the call of world interests. The flame of youth has been transformed into the radiance of age.

Where is the most beautiful description of love we know? Speaking for myself, I find it in these well-known lines: "Love suffereth long and is kind; love envieth not; love vaunteth not itself, is not puffed up, doth not behave itself unseemly, seeketh not her own, is not easily provoked, thinketh no evil; rejoiceth not in iniquity, but rejoiceth in the truth; beareth all things, believeth all things, hopeth all things, endureth all things.   Love never faileth."[5]

Now let us ask ourselves does this description fit young love or love that is matured?   Is it true that young love "suffereth long and is kind"?   I have seen some broken-hearted young lovers who did not suffer very long and some hot-headed youth who were cruel rather than kind in their zeal of love.   Is it true that youthful love "envieth not"? I have seen some young suitors looking with green-eyed envy at their more successful rivals.   Is it correct to say that young love "seeketh not its own"?   What is more possessive than youthful love's passion for its object?   Is it accurate to say of young love that it "is not easily provoked"?   What could be more fiery and sensitive?

Perhaps we have looked far enough to see that the love Paul so beautifully describes is a mellowed, ripened affection, a passion made tolerant by the memory of past mistakes, made charitable by gratitude for past forgiveness?   Love between man and woman is beautiful to behold at the marriage altar, but it has a richer sheen on a Golden Wedding anniversary.   Love between friends has a rare fineness amid the enthusiasms of a college campus, but it has an added depth after long years of sharing common burdens and responsibilities.   Social passion is splendid in the young idealist, but far more magnificent is it to keep the charitableness

---

[5] 1 Corinthians 13: 4-8.

of brotherhood into a truly liberal old age. Love of God is a warming experience in the first flush of a youthful convert's zeal, but it is far more satisfying in the heart of a veteran, who after long years in the service of his Lord can say: "I know whom I have believed, and am persuaded that he is able to keep that which I have committed unto him against that day."[6]

After a crushing political defeat, Gladstone on one occasion rose to speak with buoyant confidence, saying, "Time is on our side." We, too, may have time for an ally.

---

[6] 2 Timothy 1: 12.

X

John Sutherland Bonnell:
The Gospel for
An Age of Tension

Ours has been called an age of tension, an age of anxiety, an age of fear. The evidences are everywhere. The tempo of our lives has increased to such an extent that some cannot stand the strain. Every newspaper has its stories of international unrest and personal misfortune. The statistics of crime, delinquency, divorce, and alcoholism continue to mount. All these are indications of a condition that exists in our time and culture. There are many other people whose stories are not in the newspapers but who do not get the full satisfaction from life, who feel inadequate, dissatisfied, or defeated. Ernest Groves, the sociologist, used to say that if we want to get a picture of our time, we should stand on the downtown corner of a busy intersection in any of our large cities during the rush hour and watch the faces of the people as they pass by. He said that here you see hurry, tension, worry, anxiety everywhere. This is not true of all, for such statements can be overemphasized, but it is a real issue. It was with such people in mind that Dr. John Sutherland Bonnell spoke on the subject, "Living without Inner Tension."

He had a unique background for the ministry. As a young man he served as an attendant in the wards of a mental hospital of which his father was the superintendent. Here, he

said, was his apprenticeship to the ministry. At present he
is pastor of the Fifth Avenue Presbyterian Church in New
York City and for several years has preached regularly over
a national radio chain. He combines his public ministry
with an extensive program of personal counseling. Here he
utilizes the resources of both psychology and religion. A
leader in the pastoral psychology movement, his own methods and philosophy have been described in such books as
Pastoral Psychiatry and *Psychology for Pastor and People.*
It is his conviction, as he states in the concluding sentence of
this sermon, that there is found in the Christian gospel the
"secret of living victoriously in an age of pressure, fear and
tension."

LIVING WITHOUT INNER
TENSION [1]

By John Sutherland Bonnell

Some years ago a notable address was delivered at the Academy of Medicine in New York by Doctor G. Canby Robinson, of the Johns Hopkins Hospital at Baltimore. His subject was "The Patient as a Person." For all too long, he said, medical science had so concentrated on the study of disease that it had lost sight of the patient. It had neglected the environmental and emotional factors in illness. Then he added the significant statement that the Johns Hopkins clinic had experimentally discovered that even "the illness of a patient with organic disease could be caused by emotional tension." A dramatic change has occurred in the treatment of patients when each is now regarded as an entity of body, mind, and spirit which act and react one upon the other. In other words, the patient is now regarded as a person.

Doctor Robinson went on to describe a case history from the clinic. He hold of a man who had come to him with a serious heart condition. He received an electro-cardiograph examination and X-ray tests, and as a result of all the tests he was advised to give up his work immediately and to avoid all exertion. The prognosis was exceedingly discouraging, offering little more than a life of invalidism. About a year later Doctor Robinson received a report from

[1]Reprinted by permission from the December, 1954, issue of *Pastoral Psychology*. Copyright 1954 by Pastoral Psychology Press, Great Neck, N. Y.

one of the case-workers of the clinic that this man was showing
great improvement, that he was doing light work and
shortly expected to do heavier work. He was called in
again, and the same series of tests was made. Doctor Robinson said: "To our amazement, we were unable to discover
the slightest symptom of the disease that seemed so marked
twelve months earlier. I asked the man: 'What have you
been doing in the last twelve months?' 'Well,' he said,
'the future didn't look very bright for me. I had nothing
else to do, so I took up what I haven't done for a long time.
I began to read my Bible. As I read it, the serenity and
peace of God came into my life, and little by little I found
that I was improving.' " Doctor Robinson added: "We
discharged the man as cured." At the time he delivered
the lecture the patient was carrying on his normal occupation.

This is not an isolated instance. I believe that one of the
most important developments in the field of religion in the
second half of the twentieth century will be a recognition of
the far-reaching effects of spiritual therapy, the discovery
that faith combined with spiritual discipline possesses, along
with the help of medical science, great and beneficent power.
Both medicine and faith are agencies of God for human
healing. So we find the writer of Ecclesiasticus saying:
"Honor a physician according to the need of him with the
honors due unto him: for verily the Lord hath created
him, for from the Most High cometh healing."

Now, if all this is true of organic illnesses how much more
does it apply to those inner strains and tensions that in-
capacitate men and women and rob them of their serenity
and peace. One often hears brain workers say: "My brain
is tired from prolonged concentration on my work." But

that explanation is no longer valid. Some one is always robbing us of our comforting "alibis." Science tells us that it is practically impossible to fatigue the human brain. So we are driven to find another explanation of our weariness. How, then, are we to account for the physical, as well as the mental, exhaustion that often overtakes us when the only physical effort we may make is to sit at a desk for eight hours, with brief intermissions? Let one of the better-known medical scientists answer this question. He says: "One hundred per cent of the fatigue of the sedentary worker, in good health, is due to emotional factors . . ."

Modern psychologists have seldom blazed trails that were unknown to Professor William James of Harvard. Half a century ago Professor James wrote this: "Neither the nature nor the amount of work is accountable for the frequency and severity of our breakdowns, but their cause lies rather in those absurd feelings of hurry . . . in that breathlessness and tension, that anxiety of feature, that solicitude of result, and that lack of inner harmony and ease by which the work, with us, is apt to be accompanied."

It is not our work that wears us down; it is the destructive emotional accompaniments of labor, and the deadliest of all of these are worries, fears, and hates. It is probably more true of Americans than of any other people that we have never learned to relax as we work. As a consequence, we waste a great deal of energy which should be used much more profitably, since every taut muscle is a working muscle.

A little time ago I rode in a taxi up Fifth Avenue at the rush hour. We were caught in a traffic jam, and for fifteen minutes I experienced that exquisite torture that comes to any one possessed of Scotch blood when seeing the cash indicator steadily spinning and the wheels of the taxi not making a single turn. Just as we began to move, another taxi shot through a small opening between us and a bus and moved in front of us. My driver pulled up alongside the other taxi and very slowly and deliberately opened the window beside him. He addressed what he considered to be appropriate remarks to the driver of the other taxi. The adjectives were especially impressive. When we resumed our journey he became more and more jittery, muttering all the while to himself and cursing the other driver. He was burning up energy like a furnace while just sitting at the wheel of his car. Finally I said: "Driver, I have an important appointment right now with an out-of-town psychiatrist, and I wanted especially to be there right on the dot, and I am already twenty minutes late." He broke in: "I am sorry, Mister, but I can't help it. I am going just as fast as I can." "I know that," I said, "you don't understand me. I mentioned this fact only to remind you that I am the one who ought to be doing all the worrying in this taxi. You are the one who is making money now. Some time ago I saw that I was going to be late and that there wasn't a thing that I could do about it. I just relaxed and left the outcome in the hands of God. Why don't you try that some time?" He made no reply. Later, as I was leaving the taxi, the driver said to me very quietly: "I am sorry, Mister, that I got so excited out there on the Avenue. I have learned something today that I am not going to forget."

In every walk of life, especially in our great cities, men and women return home at night worn with fatigue. In their intensity they have lavished the very marrow of their lives. The strain is killing; the pace is murderous. They are wearing themselves out, not by overwork, but with destructive emotions manifested in disturbing conflicts with other people, in worry, and in hyper-tension.

Let us remember, however, that feverish, distracted, tense living is not a problem confined to cities or to the twentieth century. It was even true in Jesus' day. It has been true of every age. It is a characteristic of man's frailty. On one occasion the disciples of Jesus returned to report to Him the results of their preaching mission. They had experienced unlooked-for-success. The multitude, drawn together by the excitement, thronged them. Jesus looked at these fevered, tired, and excited ambassadors of His and said to them: "Come ye yourselves apart into a solitary place and rest awhile." Mark adds: "There were many coming and going and they had no leisure so much as to eat."

Our Lord and His disciples crossed the Sea of Galilee by boat. They found a quiet retreat under the trees. There, surrounded by an expanse of green grass and flowers, they united in fellowship with God. Their bodies were relaxed and their souls restored. There the disciples were given the opportunity to establish a balance between the inward and the outward. The crowd and the excitement had externalized their lives. Outer things had become so clamorous and so obtrusive that the inner "still small voice" could no longer be heard.

"When we deliberately come apart from the world," says Doctor Jowett, "the pressure of external circumstances is relaxed and we are alone. The veil of the temporal parts asunder, and we are in the Holy of Holies, and we know ourselves to be in the presence of God." It is the law of life that retirement and silence are the true secret of productivity and strength. Thomas Carlyle in his lecture "The Hero as Prophet" calls attention to the undeniable influence of solitude in fortifying human character.

It was not an accident that Moses spent forty years in the wilderness as a shepherd, for, as he engaged in this humble vocation, from the vast, unpeopled solitudes and from the everlasting stars shining so steadfastly in the canopy of heaven, there came to him that poise and inner calm and those qualities of leadership that enabled him to take a band of slaves fleeing out of Egypt and weld them into a nation.

Likewise, on the Judean hillside, the shepherd boy, David, kept watch over his father, Jesse's, flock by night. The silence of the lonely hills spoke to him of eternal things and of God, and enabled him to cultivate those spiritual insights that appear in his incomparable Psalms which have brought comfort and solace to men and women of every generation.

> The Lord is my shepherd, I shall not want;
> He maketh me to lie down in green pastures,
> He leadeth me beside the still waters,
> He restoreth my soul.

These meaningful words are the fruits of solitude.

Jesus, too, often slipped quietly away from the crowds and even from His own disciples, to find in some natural seclusion sweet communion with the Heavenly Father. When He returned from the mountainside where on one occasion He had spent a whole night in prayer with God, it is recorded that "The multitude sought to touch him, for power issued from him." He had become a perfect channel of Divine power that made Him not only invincible in Himself, but issued from Him to bless and strengthen other lives.

The wise man or woman is the one who sets apart a time in every day for waiting upon God, for reading His word, for finding His marching orders for the day. One verse of Scripture that is directed to your inner needs will keep you steadfast throughout a trying day, and will enable you to draw upon hidden springs of refreshment, serenity, and peace. Those who are neglectful of such spiritual resources are like a man journeying through the arid desert who thoughtlessly casts away the bottle of precious water on which his life will depend.

One summer night some years ago at a conference retreat I talked with a brother-minister. We climbed the side of a high hill and rested under the trees, with only the sound of the whispering leaves in our ears, and the stars of heaven overhead. Said the minister: "I want to tell you tonight about the greatest turning point in my life. I had undertaken a tremendous responsibility that was beyond my poor powers. On all sides were difficulties. One Sunday morning as I sat in a hotel bedroom I was overcome with a sense of frustration and failure and defeat. Almost irresistibly I was tempted to surrender to despair. I fell upon my knees and called upon God for help. As if in answer these words began to repeat themselves in my mind: 'Behold, my servant whom I uphold . . . my servant whom I uphold.' The words were vaguely familiar, and I hurried to the church and consulted my Concordance. I found them in the forty-second chapter of Isaiah:

"Behold, my servant whom I uphold, mine elect, in whom my soul delighteth. I have put my spirit upon him. . . . He shall not fail nor be discouraged till we have set judgment in the earth. . . . I the Lord have called thee in righteousness and will hold thy hand and will keep thee."

There was a long pause, and the minister said again: "That was one of the greatest moments of my life. Divine strength simply poured into me till I became a re-created man," and then he added solemnly: "Before God I declare unto you that in all the years that have followed, and despite many difficulties, never again have I been mastered by a sense of disappointment or failure." This minister has been used of God to bless a multitude of lives.

A basic need for all of us is to learn the secret of living victoriously in an age of pressure, fear and tension.

XI

George Buttrick:
Preacher, Pastor, and Scholar

George Buttrick has distinguished himself in many fields: as preacher, pastor, teacher, churchman, author, lecturer, and scholar. In all of these fields he has achieved some eminence, in some of them national recognition. He has had extensive experience in the pastorate, having served churches in Illinois, Vermont, and Buffalo, New York, before going to Madison Avenue Presbyterian Church, in New York City, where he served for twenty-seven years. He has held many influential positions, including the presidency of the Federal Council of Churches (now the National Council) and as Lyman Beecher lecturer at Yale University Divinity School.

When he was still a student in England, he received honors in philosophy and has been recognized as one of the keenest minds in the American pulpit and one of the most scholarly preachers. His ability as a scholar has expressed itself in a series of influential books. *The Parables of Jesus* is accepted as a standard work. His Yale lectures appeared under the title *Jesus Came Preaching*. His book *Prayer* is regarded as one of the truly significant books of our day. He has also published several other volumes. One of his most noteworthy achievements has been in serving as editor-in-chief of *The Interpreter's Bible,* a multivolume comprehensive commentary on the Scriptures that will be a standard reference in theological schools and pastors' studies for years to come.

It seems incredible that one could do so many things and still find time to do any pastoral work at all, but he did. He said that he never found any substitute for pastoral care, including pastoral calling—a task that is not easy in a city like New York and in a congregation that included both tenements and fashionable apartments. While many looked down on such futile tasks as "the ringing of doorbells," he said that he had found that even a calling card left in the hands of an apartment-house doorman may bring a man "to his minister to seek counsel or to give release to a pent-up soul." In his lectures on preaching he said that the minister should seek both the method and the mind of Jesus. Jesus, he pointed out, always held a reverence for the person. "He did not seek the crowd; He sought the individual and the crowd sought Him."[1]

Buttrick's career reminds one of Richard Baxter, famous preacher of England of the seventeenth century. In addition to his preaching, he was very active in the affairs of his day, saw every family in his parish of some eight hundred families once a year and still managed to publish more than one hundred volumes.

At the present time Dr. Buttrick is university preacher at Harvard University and professor of Christian morals. We have included here a sermon from his earlier years at Madison Avenue Presbyterian Church. He takes his text from the ancient Book of Kings, but he is soon talking about life on Wall Street and in Atlantic City, and deals with the problem of finding unity in life.

---

[1]Buttrick, From *Jesus Came Preaching*, Scribners, 1936, p. 118.

GOD OF THE HILLS AND VALLEYS

By George Arthur Buttrick

> *And a man of God came near and spake unto
> the King of Israel, and said: Thus saith Je-
> hovah: Because the Syrians have said, Jehovah
> is a god of the hills, but he is not a god of the
> valleys; therefore will I deliver all this great
> multitude into thy hand, and ye shall know that
> I am Jehovah.*
>
> —1 Kings xx: 28.

A superstition interests us for these reasons: first, it is
fantastic—like a man on stilts; second, it is old-fashioned
and enables us to feel superior—as when we laugh at a
woman wearing the styles of twenty years ago; third (though
this reason we are slow to admit) there are traces of it remaining in us, and it reveals us to ourselves.

Here then is a superstition. Each tribe of old had its god:
the Moabites had Chemosh, the Israelites had Jehovah, the
Philistines had Baal. Victory in battle meant that the god
of the conquering tribe was more powerful than his neigh-
bor gods. Israel had conquered, which fact proved the
strength of Jehovah. But the defeated Syrians had noticed
that all the altars of Jehovah were built on hilltops. Perhaps
Israel had seen altar-smoke always ascending, had argued
therefore that God was "up," and accordingly had built
altars as near His dwelling-place as possible; or perhaps hilltops seemed sacred to them for the vague reasons for which
they still seem so to us. Whatever the cause, their shrines
were hilltop-shrines. So the Syrians naively concluded that

God was only on the hills: if they attacked on the plains they could circumvent the might of Israel's Jehovah. So the answer, which also has its traces of superstition:

> Thus saith Jehovah: Because the Syrians have said, Jehovah is a god of the hills, but he is not a god of the valleys; therefore will I deliver all this great multitude into thy hand, and ye shall know that I am Jehovah.

I

Fantastic? Yes. Primitive? Yes. With its traces in us still? I fear me, yes. Jesus met a woman who told Him: "The Jews say that God is to be worshipped at Jerusalem, and the Samaritans say that He is in this mountain"; and He, knowing full well that superstitions die hard, told her: "God is Spirit." Yet the naive faith clings that God is here —in a church, but not there—on the Atlantic City boardwalk or in Wall Street; He is now—on Sunday, but not then—on next Saturday afternoon. When we pause to think, we realize that God is a Presence—the thought of our thought, the light of our light. But we do not often pause to think. So for most of us God is only on the hilltops of sacred influence, and not on the plains of daily life. And what we do not realize, even when we pause to think, is that this assumption that God is limited to times and places (we being the modern Syrians) is as ruinous now as in olden years: we are thereby delivered into the hands of our foes.

But why should this divided loyalty be ruinous? Frankly, people do not regard it as ruinous: it is an accepted practice. Abraham Lincoln deemed it ruinous: "No nation can exist half-slave and half-free"—but he gave no reason for his conviction. Jesus deemed it ruinous: "No man can serve

two masters"—and He gave a reason at least by implication;
"for," said He, "either he will love the one and hate the
other," swayed by his heart's devotion; "or he will hold to
the one and despise the other," swayed by self-interest. Then
He added emphatically: "Ye cannot serve God and Mammon." Either we love God in the heart's deep loyalty, or
we cling to Mammon in a mistaken self-interest.

So the piercing insight of Jesus leads to the reason why a
divided life is ruinous: Our nature is a unity; any cleavage
in us is our hurt. If a man in the summer is asked by his
wife to beat carpets he is probably unhappy at the task.
Why? Because his mind is divided: while he is beating
carpets he is thinking of the thing he would rather do; and
consequently the work seems much harder than it really is.
But if he were on the way to the golf course he would be
happy, though there he probably expends just as much
energy as when beating carpets; but there his mind is un-
divided. A cut hand bleeds and throbs: the nature is divided. Religion on Sunday and no religion on Monday:
the spirit bleeds, actually if invisibly, for then the spirit is
divided! . . . whereas constitutionally it is ordained a unity.

Moreover (and here again the insight of Jesus is our
light), a divided nature is always in movement towards one
of its loyalties. "Either he will love the one and hate the
other" (either it is travelling Godwards), "or he will hold
to the one and despise the other" (or it is travelling earthwards). And—here is the rapier thrust of the truth of
Christ—if it is not consciously travelling Godwards, it is by
default travelling earthwards. Or, to use the picturesque
language of this text, if the hills are not subduing the valleys,
the valleys are levelling the hills. For it is not in human

nature to remain divided. Nitroglycerin is an explosive because its constituents (nitric acid, sulphuric acid, and glycerin) naturally do not belong together: a slight blow will send each element hurtling to its proper company. Earthworship and God-worship do not cohabit. Sometimes there is an explosion—and the whole nature is wrecked: the wreckage can be seen in our law-courts and our morgues. But, wreckage or no wreckage, our nature is moving ever one way or another: it cannot remain divided. In a deeper sense than we usually speak the words, "It is against the constitution"!

II

Yet see how an ancient superstition persists: *there are the hilltops of the sacred and the plains of the secular.* That division is in the very words. "Secular" comes from the Latin "seculum": "what is of man, of earth, of time." The heavens are *there,* and God is there: the earth is *here:* a gulf is set.

Of course business is necessary. Worship itself is not possible in our climate without a roof—and a roof spells business. Nor could we desire to worship if we lacked food—and food again spells business. Labor and the exchange of goods are in realest sense divine: for they are essential to a sovereign life. When we examine with care the parables of Jesus we see clearly, by His repeated references, that the realm of toil and trade are much in His thought. Fidelity and skill there won His instant admiration. But when the moods which govern worship, the ethic of the mount, do not consciously sway business, business unconsciously becomes earthy. If trade does not wittingly honor God it unwittingly "holds to" Mammon.

Gangsterism has its orbit round a money motive—with, perhaps, as a lesser impelling a base desire to strut and domineer. Graft in city government has its orbit round a money motive. Bootleggism and clip-joints have their orbit round a money motive. Brokerage houses of the wrong kind (those of the right kind are as right and necessary as any branch of trade)—brokerage houses which on one telephone recommend the selling of a given stock and on another telephone at the same time advise its purchase—have their orbit round a money motive. And so does short selling. And so does our sex-soaked movie-traffic. And so do our advertisement-infested radio programs. Even if these pursuits were not destructive, even if they did not provoke our indignation, they would still provoke our pity. We would still be moved to say to them what Tennyson said to a young lady who had described a certain marriage as "penniless;" the poet loudly slapped down one penny on the table and as emphatically remarked: "There: I give you that. That is the God you worship."

In all these instances we see business, which in itself is of a divine purpose, assuming that God is limited to a hill. Its loyalties are divided, but they do not stay divided. Because business in these instances does not consciously love God, it unconsciously (for this money-love is not at first deliberate) drifts towards Mammon. It becomes earthy by deafult. The Syrian superstition takes on new life, and—tell me if I speak not truth!—the Syrian doom has come upon us: we are smitten hip and thigh. Neither God nor man can ever be divided, either in themselves or from one another. The universe is a universe: one life, one song! It bleeds if it is cut.

III

Illustrations are not far to seek: *God, we say, is on the hilltops of individual allegiance, but He is not on the plains of national and international dealings.* We speak of the "individual gospel" and the "social gospel," but these two are joined together—and let "no man put asunder"! There would be no lake of social life without the inflowing of individual springs; and, conversely, no man could be a man without his neighbors. Even a hermit has learned from his comrades how to gather food and fashion clothes and make a shelter—and is therefore in no full sense a hermit.

Let it be granted that your relationship and mine with a man in Timbuktu or Tasmania is not immediately clear. Yet it is daily becoming clearer. Our newspapers retail the gossip of the world. A depression in America occasions a revolution in Siam. The radio picks up the ends of the earth and ties them in a knot at the end of every room. The Pullman Company kindly supplies a little folder to advise us that the materials of the car in which we are riding came from everywhere—from Beersheba, and the land of the Chaldees, and the unprofitable isles of the sea.

But the Christian outlook, though it is still far from regulating individual life, has much more influence there than on the farflung stage of international policy. We have little respect for a man who "has a chip on his shoulder," but what is called "national honor" is on the alert for the lightest affront. Duelling is indecent between individuals, but war between nations can somehow still be splendid. The frontier rule of "pistols for two and coffee for one" has gone from among men (it is plain barbarous), but among nations it is still taken for granted. Forgiveness between neighbors is counted a virtue—but forgiveness among nations would be a gross sentimentalism.

In short, Christ may live here (on our separate points of rock), but He cannot live there on the widespreading plains where all the world is woven into one web of life. "Therefore will I deliver all this great multitude" into the doom of suicidal strife! God grant that recent American initiative—a gleam of light in every truth—may guide the nations out of their Syrian superstition into a Christlike day!

IV

We have yet to instance the most common and the most serious of our attempts to limit God: *He is on the conspicuous hilltops of external conduct, but not in the hidden valleys of imagination and desire.*

Mankind has always known that our consciousness is in two realms which are yet one: private thought and public deed. But psychology has recently introduced us to the idea of the subconscious. Below private thought, below the recognized motive and wish there is a dim realm of memory, habit, disposition and inheritance which, though uncharted, profoundly affects our whole experience. Thus a woman may have an unreasoning fear of death because of some childhood experience which, though it may no longer be in clear memory, is still at work in the subconscious. Perhaps the psychologists are attributing more than a proportionate influence to the subconscious, but it is proven at any rate that our invisible character has vaster bounds and more mysterious depths than we have dreamed.

The mind is like New York City at night seen from afar: there are vivid towers and pinnacles corresponding to our words and deeds; there are partly illumined walls, corresponding to our known resolves and imaginings; and below all there are houses and streets and tunnels in the darkness where

ever a multitudinous life proceeds, corresponding to the subconscious. Beyond cavil our hidden life is far more vital
and determinative than other generations have believed.

But it is from these valleys that we have tried to keep God.
We are all more circumspect in conduct than in desire. We
would not strike with our fists someone whom we dislike, but
we do strike him in our angry thoughts. Our deed may not
be shameful, but the imagination is not unstained! God is
God of the conspicuous hills, but He is not God of the
hidden valleys.

Yet the self cannot thus be divided. Either the seemly
conduct will by fervent prayer subdue the secret life, or the
unseemly desire will burst into sight to disgrace the conduct.
We say of a man that he "suddenly went wrong" in theft or
treachery or fleshliness. No man "suddenly goes wrong."
His life has been long divided—worthiness in the seen, un-
worthiness in the unseen—but it cannot stay divided. It is
on the move towards one loyalty or the other—and the secret
darkness at last breaks through to destroy the light of conduct. The doom of the Syrians is come upon him! Because
he has said God is the God of the hills but he is not God
of the valleys he is given over to a self-ordained destruction.

V

I am pleading that our Christianity shall not be merely a
Sabbath tassel on the common robe, but a devotion that
throbs at the heart and tingles like life-blood to the finger tips.

I am pleading that it shall not be circumscribed by individual witness, but be courageously applied to business,
politics and statescraft.

I am pleading, above all that it shall not be kept only in
the light, but move and reign also in that unseen potent

world of desire and image and resolve. A man's real religion is what he does with his aloneness—and afterwards what his aloneness does with him.

It is not a matter of imitating Jesus: He did not live in our age. Nor is it a matter even of asking "What would Jesus do?" It is rather a matter of keeping His picture before us always, everywhere—speaking or dreaming, voting or toiling, pleasuring or reading—and constantly praying that His Spirit may animate us through and through. The divided life bleeds—for it is cut! The united life sings like a river flowing to the sea, like an organ in some vast "Amen,"—as Jesus sang as He went to a Cross!

XII

Robert McCracken:
Facing People's Questions

Robert McCracken has had the unenviable job of following Dr. Harry Emerson Fosdick in the pulpit of Riverside
Church in New York City. Before going to Riverside
Church he held pastorates in Edinburgh and Glasgow, and
served as professor of Christian Theology and Philosophy at
McMaster University. He has published one volume of sermons which were preached in Riverside Church and which
carry on the same tradition of speaking to people's practical
needs that that pulpit had known under his predecessor. In
fact, his philosophy of preaching as expressed in the preface
of this volume reveals a philosophy similar to that of Dr.
Fosdick's. "Life-situation preaching," Dr. McCracken says,
is that preaching in which

> the preacher finds the point of departure in a real,
> contemporary problem. It may be social or per-
> sonal; it may be theological or ethical or psycho-
> logical. Whatever it is, his first business is to get
> at the core of it, and, that done, to seek as cogently
> and helpfully as he knows how, to work out the
> solution, with the mind and spirit of Jesus and the
> Biblical revelation the constant points of reference
> and direction.[1]

---

[1]From *Questions People Ask,* by Robert McCracken, copyrighted 1951 by Harper
& Brothers. Used by permission.

With this philosophy in the background, he preached a series of sermons on "The Questions People Ask." He included a wide range of questions, all the way from "Is There an Art to Living in New York City?" to "Can We Believe in a Personal God?" All of them grew out of his "everyday contact with people" and the problems they have presented. He says that questions are inevitable. They vary from person to person and from generation to generation, but if religion is a real issue, it is bound to raise questions. Some of them are basic questions that have "to do with the existence and character of God, the nature and destiny of man, the relation of man to his Maker and to his fellows." For some people the facing of these questions is an urgent business. For some it is difficult. Some have to do battle for their faith. "These sermons," he said, "were preached with such people in mind. They represent an attempt to come to grips with the religious and moral difficulties confronting men and women in the modern world, first by facing each difficulty frankly and openly, and then by bringing to bear on it Christian insights and applications."[2]

We have chosen here a sermon that deals with one of the most basic questions of life, "Can Human Nature Be Changed?"

---

[2]Ibid.

CAN HUMAN NATURE BE CHANGED?[1]

By Robert McCracken

Dick Sheppard used to tell a story about a man who sat drinking in a bar. He had been drinking for a long time. He had swallowed considerable quantities of liquor. And as he drank, he wept. He wept because he had wasted his life. He wept because he had failed to do his duty by his family. He wept because he had never appreciated his wife properly. He wept because somehow his good intentions always went wrong. But never mind, he told himself, this time it would be different. He would redeem the past and make up for everything. All, he resolved, would yet be well. He felt uplifted and noble at the very thought. His mind glowed with a genial assurance of virtue. Just then the bartender said, "Time, gentlemen, please"—*and he went home and swore at his wife.*

Can anything be done for a man like that, a man whose intentions are honourable but whose performances are lamentable? He wants to be a better man, but what do his wishes amount to? He is to-day substantially what he was a year ago; he has the same old and apparently inveterate faults and failings. Indeed, the chances are that instead of improving he has grown worse, is weaker in will and grosser in desire. Is there anything that can bring about a change in him and so transform his whole nature as to make him what, in his best moments, he fain would be?

[1]From *Questions People Ask*, copyrighted 1951 by Harper & Brothers. Used by permission.

Some people are emphatically of the opinion that nothing can be done. Any chance of reforming an individual beyond the period of adolescence is simply hopeless. By then the faults of temper and temperament are too deeply embedded in the character to be rooted out and destroyed. They are as much a part of the individual as his skin. He may spruce himself up a bit, apply a little polish here, work down an excrescence there, but the main outline and quality of his character—nothing can alter that.

A newspaper columnist, whose views are read by hundreds of thousands and whose name is a household word, recently, and in forthright fashion, expressed the point thus: "If a man is a philanderer, he will be a philanderer to the end. It is only in novels that a miracle occurs in the last chapter that makes the drunkard reform and become sober, the grouch sunny and sweet-tempered, the miser generous and open-handed, the shrew so mild that butter wouldn't melt in her mouth. In real life these things never happen. People continue to be what habit and usage have made them."

There is nothing vague or ambiguous about that viewpoint, but if it is clear-cut and dogmatic, it is also dreadfully dismal and pessimistic, and one wonders whether those who propound it or who subscribe to it have really thought out in terms of strict logic its implications and consequences. We are all weary and sick of the world we know, a world of fear and hate and greed and slaughter. We are all longing and hoping for a new world, a world that will guarantee justice and security, quietness and peace. But with the passing of every day it becomes increasingly evident that we shall never have and never preserve a new world unless and until fear and hate and greed and pride are purged from human hearts. According to the view just described, such a purge is impossible. Human nature cannot be changed. Nothing can be done for a person if years of habit, or of environment, or of heredity, have bent his character into one shape, and that shape is crooked or deformed. The drunkard will always be a drunkard. The sensualist will always be a sensualist. The world will always be at the mercy of crooks and gangsters and upstart dictators.

It is a dreadfully dismal and pessimistic conclusion to be driven to, and it is made so much the more so when one thinks not—as we have been doing up to this point—of single individuals but of humanity at large. For consider what such a conclusion involves. There is no abiding or ultimate cure for the ills of humanity. Nothing can be done permanently to heal its hurt. In human nature there is an incorrigible element which means that history is bound to go on repeating itself to the end. Because of the terrible things that have been happening in the world since the opening of the century, because of the disappointed hopes and disillusionment that have followed in the wake of two world wars, people in all ranks of life are capitulating, or are under heavy pressure to capitulate, to depression and despair. I quote from a notable speech made by Mr. Winston Churchill in the autumn of 1946: "Certainly the scene we survey bears many uncomfortable resemblances to that of 1938. Indeed, in some respects, it is even darker. The peoples of Europe have fallen immeasurably deeper into the pit of misery and confusion. Many of their cities are in ruins. Millions of their homes have been destroyed. They have torn one another into pieces with more ferocity, on a larger scale, and with more deadly weapons than ever before. But have they found stable and lasting peace? Is the brotherhood of mankind any nearer? Has the reign of law returned? Alas, although the resources and vitality of nearly all the European countries are woefully diminished, many of their old hatreds burn on with undying flame. Skeletons with gleaming eyes . . . glare at each other across the ashes and rubble heap of what was once the august Roman Empire and later a Christian civilization. Is there never to be an end? Is there no salvation here below? Are we to sink through gradations of infinite suffering to primordial levels—

> A discord. Dragons of the prime,
> That tear each other in their slime

or can we avoid our doom?"

Can we avoid our doom? Can human nature be changed? Can man's ethical capacity catch up with his scientific skill? In one form or another, that is the question of the hour. Statesmen are asking it. Scientists are asking it. Philosophers and educationists and churchmen are asking it. And the man on the street, as he reads his newspaper and listens to the radio and talks with his friends, is asking it, too. Is there a way out of the muddle we are in? Is there any salvation here below? Is evil so endemic in human nature as to be incurable, or is there a remedy, a sovereign remedy for it?

Did I say that is the question of the hour? It is the question of the ages. There is nothing new about such a question. In century after century men have asked it. But there is this to bear in mind. Deep down in the human heart there is something that refuses to take "No" as the answer. The pessimists and cynics, like the poor, are always with us, and they and their positions have to be reckoned with and not ignored, but they are never really in the majority. "Hope springs eternal in the human breast." "Man," as Nietzsche

said, "is a recurring decimal." You can never work him out.
You may divide and divide to your heart's content, but each
figure you get, so far from being the end is simply a new beginning. There is something invincible and indestructible in
man. The visions he cherishes may become dim but they do
not die. The torch is handed on from generation to generation. Even when the night is at its darkest the song may be
heard—

> These things shall be,—a loftier race
> Than ere the world hath known shall rise
> With flame of freedom in their souls,
> And light of knowledge in their eyes.

Mark that last line—"And light of knowledge in their
eyes." It offers a clue to the hopes of so many. If they
refuse to despair of human nature or of the possibility of
achieving a new and better order, it is because of what they
believe knowledge can do, provided only that it is given a
chance and on a big enough scale—the ignorance it can dis-
pel, the prejudice it can overcome, the miraculous transfor-
mation it can work both in the broadening and elevating of
men's minds and in the refining and enriching of their characters. That is the case for education as one of the cures—
there are those who think it is the major cure—for the ills
of humanity. Presented at its best, it is a strong case. It
is being advocated with passionate faith and conviction by
men and women who see civilization engaged in a race with
catastrophe and who are desperate to avert a crash. There
are some things one notices about that advocacy. One is the
growing tendency to acknowledge and deplore the diminu-
tion of spiritual values in the contemporary world bound up
with training of a purely vocational character. As a scientist
remarked not long ago, if education is wholly given over to
specialization on vocationally useful pursuits it will tend to

produce young barbarians who know nothing of the rich heritage of culture and are blind outside their own narrow field. Another is the anxiety that the knowledge made available by education should be turned to constructive rather than destructive ends; that atomic energy should be used not to blast the world but to rebuild it; and as with the new physics, so with the new biology, the new chemistry, the new engineering—that instead of producing poisons capable of blotting out cities, and infections of such violence and virulence as to wipe out whole communities, and bombs destructive enough to reduce to a hideous rubble the fruits of human labour for a thousand years, the awesome power within our reach and at our command should be employed to raise the standard of living of all the peoples, to bring peace, plenty and tranquillity.

There is another thing one notices. It is the recognition on the part of many educationists that something more than education is needed if human nature is to be changed and a new and better order established. Witness the judgement of Sir Richard Livingstone, the President of Corpus Christi College, Oxford: "We and our education have been too absorbed in the matter of life to think of its spirit. We must restore to it a vitamin, deficient both there and in our life—a religion, a philosophy of living, a definite ideal to guide, discipline and dominate the lives of individuals and, through them, national life."

It is an impressive judgement. Not all are disposed to approve it. Many prefer to make legislation the ally of education. Isn't that the significance of the experiment being carried out in Soviet Russia? And Soviet Russia apart, legislation has on its credit side a long list of remarkable achievements. My background being British, I think at once

of the Repeal of the Corn Laws under Cobden, of the introduction of the Factory Acts associated with the name of
Lord Shaftesbury, of the emancipation of the slaves in the
West Indies and of Wilberforce's labours to make it effective
by statute. I have no doubt that you, for your part, are
thinking of events no less striking in America's story. Nor
need attention be confined to the past. No one can deny
that wise, impartial, farsighted legislation is needed now if
catastrophe is to be averted; it is needed on a world-wide
scale. And in the case of the United Nations it is being set
up—slowly, laboriously, painfully under our very eyes here
in New York City. We are the witnesses of an attempt
which has for its goal nothing less than a radical, thorough-
going change in human nature, and which merits the constant and vigilant support of men and women of good will
everywhere.

And yet our real problem lies deeper—deeper than either
education or legislation. There is a passage in Trotsky's
Literature and Revolution which makes pathetic reading,
especially in view of Trotsky's end. He is writing about the
change of spirit to become manifest with the establishment of
the Communist Revolution. "All the emotions which we
revolutionists at the present time feel apprehensive of nam-
ing—so much have they been worn thin by hypocrites—such
as disinterested friendship, love for one's neighbours, sympathy—will be the mighty ringing words of socialist poetry.
. . . All will be equally interested in the success of the whole.
There will be no running after profits. There will be nothing mean, no betrayals, no bribery, none of the things which
form the soul of competition in a society divided into
classes." What ruined that Utopia? One thing—unre-
generate human nature. We have got to get behind the
system to the men who comprise it. No legal framework, no

external organization of society, no school or college curriculum will of itself transform character or guarantee that people who before were competitive and grasping and unprincipled over night become the opposite. Behind the problem of a warless world lies the prior problem of the people who are to live in it as brothers. As Herbert Spencer put it: "There is no political alchemy by which you can get golden conduct out of leaden instincts."

Is there an alchemy by which you can get golden conduct out of leaden instincts? Yes, there is. Alongside of education and legislation there can be set another term—Regeneration. If Christianity affirms anything at all, it affirms that human nature can be changed, genuinely, radically and permanently changed. The drunkard can reform and become sober, the impure can become pure, the grouch can become genial, the individual who is plagued with temper or temperament can be helped to integrate his personality and can learn the secret of self-control, the crook and the gangster, yes, and the upstart dictator can be won to a new frame of mind and to a new way of life.

No one who appreciates the issues that are at stake here will be disposed either to ignore or to treat lightly this claim. If it is false, its falsity should be exposed. If it is true, the truth should be proclaimed as with the sound of a trumpet. It is not too much to say that Christianity stands or falls by its claim to transform human nature. As one writer expressed it, deliberately putting the thought into the most provocative form of words he could devise, "If Jesus Christ cannot make character, he can make nothing else." But he can make character. He has been making it for sixty generations. He found the nature of Zacchaeus greedy and he changed it. He found the nature of Augustine lustful and he changed it. He found the nature of Elizabeth Fry indolent and he changed it.

The evidence is from the present as well as the past. One of the glories of the Christian religion is that every day it raises up new witnesses; it produces fresh evidence of its validity and virility as it goes along. Take, for instance, the testimony of Hugh Redwood, a prominent member of the staff of the London *Daily News:* "If you should ask me by what authority I talk about the power of Christ to change human nature, I should reply to you simply (and God knows without one word or thought of boasting) because he has changed my nature. I can look anybody in the face to-day— my friends, my colleagues, and what, perhaps, is most difficult of all, the members of my own household and family—and be sure that they know, as I know, that I am really and literally a new creature in Christ Jesus since the day when he came into my life."

What do we make of that? And it is only one instance. There are so many others, all of them unanswerable arguments for Christianity. Unless for nineteen hundred years people have been combining in a vast conspiracy to talk claptrap and humbug, Christ can change and renew human nature, can solve the moral problems of existence. And the moral problems, not the political or the economic ones, are the prior and basic problems of existence. People like you and me have had their natures changed by Christ. Drunkards have become sober, misers have become generous and open-handed, tempery individuals who have made themselves and other people miserable by their tantrums have found the way to self-control. Not only in novels, but in real life these things have happened. By the grace of God and the power of Christ people have ceased to be any longer what usage and habit had made them.

What about us? Does our nature need changing? And have we found, when we have tried to change it, that we are unable to get at the seat of the trouble? The fact is that no one working singlehanded and alone can change himself. To attempt self-reform without Divine grace is to be like Sisyphus, rolling a stone uphill only to find it come down again with greater force. It is to have a bow without a sling, a sword without a blade. Henry Ward Beecher in his autobiography describes the never-to-be-forgotten morning when—to quote his own words—"I found out that it is God's nature to love man in his sin for the purpose of helping him out of it, as my mother loved me when I was in trouble that she might help me out of it. Then," he says, "I found God." That goes to the heart of the matter. The secret of a changed nature lies there.

Conclusion

The Sermon and the Service
of Worship

Any discussion of life-situation preaching would be incomplete if it did not include some reference to the service of worship of which it is a part. A sermon does not stand alone like a lecture in a classroom. Its very setting is different. It is presented in a sanctuary which is designed for the purpose of worship. There usually are present some religious symbols that remind the people of the reality of the Christian faith. The subject of this book is the sermon but the sermon is a part of a service of worship that also includes the lift of music, the inspiration of scripture, the quietness and reverence of moments of silence and prayer, all of which have values in their own right and also strengthen and support the sermon.

The sermon is prepared to meet the needs of the people. The worship service is also prepared to meet the needs of the people, some of their deepest needs. So significant are its purposes that such a man as Professor Hocking, speaking of some of life's highest values like beauty, recreation, friendship, and love, said, "Worship is the whole which includes them all."

In the hour of worship a man centers his attention upon God. He becomes conscious of the presence of God. Of course, men live in the presence of God at all times, but in the hour of worship they become more conscious of it and attempt to see life from that perspective. Worship elevates our scale of values. As Dr. Fosdick puts it, "In worship we are reminded of values that the world makes us forget." Worship purges the evil from one's life. It cleanses from all that is unworthy; it assures men of divine forgiveness and renewal. Worship creates a sense of community and fellowship, not only with the congregation in which one may be worshiping at the time, which is very important, but also with all men everywhere. Dean Sperry of Harvard said that on attending a service of worship in a famous cathedral in England it seemed tenanted by all the generations gone and all generations yet to come. The same feeling can be present in any service of worship. A man links himself with all the ages when he worships. Men have worshiped in catacombs and cathedrals, in frontier cabins and stately city churches, but they worshiped the same God and found the same resources of faith and hope. In worship men gain new insights into the possibilities of their own lives, new awareness of spiritual strength and energy. In true worship men dedicate or commit themselves to the service of God and their fellowmen, like young Isaiah coming down from the temple, saying, "Here am I, send me."

A service of worship, well-planned and conducted, can be a means of great personal help. As Howard Chandler Robbins has said, "It tranquillizes the mind, it fortifies the will, it integrates the personality." He further points out that worship exists for its own right; men worship God "in grateful acknowledgment of his reality." It should not be approached from any utilitarian point of view, but it does have great personal and social values.

Worship at its best is the highest expression of life. It must be granted that all of this does not happen in every service, and that it does not all happen to everyone who comes to church. It is true that "many attend church but few worship," but the potential is always there. This is the reason that people need to be trained to worship. The service needs to be interpreted to them so that they understand the purpose and meaning of worship.

People need to know the importance of their own attitudes. They do not go to church as they go to a football game or to a play, to watch others perform. If they go to be entertained, they will be disappointed; if they go to criticize, they will find flaws; but if they go to worship, they will find values regardless of the architecture of the room or the subject of the sermon. This is a part of life-situation preaching, to teach people to use such resources as public worship.

People need to have not only the service as a whole interpreted to them but the individual parts as well. They need to be taught how to use periods of silence and meditation. Such familiar parts of the service as the Lord's Prayer should be frequently explained for them so that they do not become a mere form. The same is true of the communion service. The offering, when it is seen as an act of commitment, has great value. It is more than the taking up of a collection; it also is an act of worship. Great hymns like "Dear Lord and Father of Mankind" or "God of Grace and God of Glory" contain complete messages in themselves and can become a real resource in daily life. If people are trained to worship, the hour is worth while no matter how inadequate the sermon. This is no argument for poorly prepared sermons; it does mean that the sermon has a great ally in the service of worship of which it is a part.

Materials that go into a service of worship should be carefully selected. Here a minister has a great opportunity. The wealth of the ages is at his disposal. The sermon is pretty much his own, and should be, but in the rest of the service he has great music to draw upon, great hymns and anthems of all generations, nationalities, and backgrounds. The whole range of Scripture, the suggestion of symbolism, the periods of silence and meditation all make real the resources and truth of the Christian faith and strengthen and support the sermon he has prepared.

Of all the elements in the service of worship, none is more important than the prayers, particularly the pastoral prayer. George Buttrick says, "If the minister had to choose between prayer and sermon he might better forget the sermon." Fortunately he does not have to make that choice. His prayer is his greatest test. Here he expresses all the moods of worship, in fact, almost all the aspects of the religious life: thanksgiving, praise, adoration, faith, confession, intercession, petition, aspiration, dedication, and commitment. We said in the introduction that the man who does not know his people cannot preach tellingly to them. So, the man who does not know his people cannot lead them effectively in prayer. To lead the people in prayer he must know the people and he must know God.

Such a responsibility requires much preparation. There are differences of opinion as to whether a man should write out his prayers in preparation. For some this makes it too formal and artificial and destroys the spirit of prayer. Each one must find his own methods in such matters, but this does not decrease the importance of preparation. It is the kind of preparation that is itself done in meditation and prayer.

We will include one of Dr. Fosdick's pastoral prayers as an example of what such a prayer can be. It includes adoration and praise, gratitude, confession, faith, intercession, and petition. It includes concern for the individual, the church, and the common good. Note that the language is the language of Scripture but also the language of the people:

Eternal spirit, in Whom we live, from Whom in vain we try to flee, grant us in Thy sanctuary now a saving experience of inner quiet, serenity, and peace, in which Thou shalt be real to us. We have been restless and overbusy in a noisy and troubled world, until we have lost our poise. We need Thee, Thou strong foundation that storms cannot shake, Thou deep well that droughts cannot exhaust, Thou inner citadel that no outward foe can seize.

Deep in our hearts remind us now of things we ought never to forget.

Recall to us our blessings, that we may be grateful. The faces of our family and friends, whom we have loved long since and lost awhile, the kindness of the living, loyal in their affection, the great heritage of the past, bought with the sacrifices of our sires, and all the daily goodness that sustains us, the opportunities that beckon us, the resources of beauty and truth that enrich us, and Christ over all, blessed forever—recall to us such sources of spiritual wealth and power, that we may be thankful.

Remind us of our sins, that we may be penitent. Here where Thy judgment of light falls upon our lives and reveals the darkness in them, save us from mean excuses and evasions. Recall our ill tempers, our resentments and infidelities, our harmful tongues, our selfish pride, our hardened hearts, our neglect of opportunity, and our contentment with trivial living—and so chasten us with sincere repentance and lead us to amendment of life.

Remind us of the hope of the world, that we may not be overborne by its disaster. Thou, Lord God Omnipotent, the beginning and the ending, art still God; before Thee no evil shall stand forever, and no lie shall triumph over truth. The kingdoms of this world shall become the Kingdom of Thy Christ, and men shall yet beat their swords into ploughshares and their spears into pruning hooks. Incorporate our faith and loyalty into that great hope, and let neither our confidence in it nor our devotion to it fail because of the fury of the wicked when they boast themselves in the day of their pride.

To this end, lift up Thy church and purify it for Thy service in this day of our need. Especially we beseech Thee for Thy people here, that we may be worthy of our vocation as a congregation of Thy disciples in these challenging days. Keep our fidelity true, our care for all sorts and conditions of people sincere, our own lives genuinely Christian, and our service effectual.

Watch over this nation, we beseech Thee, and on all who guide its destinies let Thy guidance be evident, that we may in the end be ministers of an abiding peace. And upon us, one by one, so let Thy grace come, that, facing our temptations, bearing our griefs, sustaining our anxieties, and enduring all hardships, we may be true servants of

the common good and forerunners of Thy Kingdom's coming. We pray in the Spirit of Christ.
Amen.[1]

Here, then, is the pastor's great opportunity. This is
his one great hour, when he leads in worship and when he
speaks or preaches to his people. All of his experiences of
dealing with people, one by one, are in the background as he
makes his preparation and as he comes to the responsibilities
of this service. All of his study of the Scripture, all his
reading, all his experience, all his periods of prayer and
devotion are concentrated for this service. When he steps
into the sanctuary for this high occasion he links himself
with the great tradition of men down through the generations who have led their people in the worship of God and,
to the best of their ability, have brought the light of the
gospel to the issues of their day.

---

[1]Used by permission of Dr. Fosdick.

APPENDIX I

One Hundred Sermon Titles

Below are listed one hundred sermon titles that deal with life situations. They give something of a cross section of the preaching that is being done in this area. These sermon titles are drawn from a variety of sources: from books of sermons and from journals of preaching. These are all sermons that have appeared in print; the sources have been included in case someone might wish to see how a preacher handled a certain theme. They are included here because they might be suggestive to others as to the possibilities of such an approach to preaching today.

Adams, Hampton, "Can Christianity Master Pessimism?" from Adams, *Christian Answers to War Questions,* Revell, 1943.

Atwood, Bertram de Heus, "Life's Second Best," From *The Pulpit,* June, 1944.

Austin, Eugene, "The Peril of Conformity," from *The Pulpit,* October, 1952.

Bell, Bernard Iddings, "The Need to Love," from Bell, *God Is Not Dead,* Harper & Brothers, 1945.

Blackwelder, Oscar, "What Machinery May Do to People," from *The Pulpit,* September, 1951.

Blackwood, Andrew, "Praying About Your Thorn in the Flesh," from *Pulpit Digest,* July, 1954.

Brooks, William E., "A Living Faith—A Living Force," from *The Pulpit,* June, 1946.

Burkhart, Roy, "Perils of the Average Person," from *Pulpit Digest,* August, 1955.

Chappell, Clovis, "Hope for the Handicapped," from *The Pulpit,* October, 1950.

214

Cleverdon, Leroy A., "The Church in the City," from *The Pulpit,* September, 1946.

Conover, C. Eugene, "Face Life with Courage," from *The Pulpit,* October, 1955.

Davis, Denver Jackson, "How You Can Fashion Your Future," from *Pulpit Digest,* June, 1955.

Davis, Harrison, "Overcoming Littleness," from *Pulpit Digest,* December, 1955.

Deems, Mervin, "When Life Loses Its Zest," from *The Pulpit,* June, 1950.

de Velder, Marion, "When Life Kicks Back," from *The Pulpit,* August, 1946.

Drew, George, "Can You Stand Being an Average Person?" from *The Pulpit,* February, 1951.

Dunnington, Lewis L., "What Is Your Goal?" from Dunnington, *Handles of Power,* Abingdon, 1942.

Edwards, K. Morgan, "The Conquest of Doubt," from *The Pulpit,* August, 1948.

Fagerburg, Frank, "For Those Ready to Quit," from *The Pulpit,* April, 1953.

Feldman, Abraham, "The Best Years of Our Lives," from *The Pulpit,* January, 1948.

Ferry, John G., "The Comfort of God," from *The Pulpit,* September, 1955.

Foote, Gaston, "Making the Most of It," from *The Pulpit,* September, 1951.

Frank, Melvin, "Vacation Temptations," from *The Pulpit,* July, 1953.

Gilkey, Charles, "Religion as Refuge—And as Challenge," from Gilkey, *Perspectives,* Harper & Brothers, 1933.

Gilkey, James Gordon, "The Sources of Surplus Power in Human Life," from Newton, ed., *Best Sermons of 1924,* Harcourt, Brace & Co., 1924.

Gossip, Arthur J., "A Message for Grey Days," from Gossip, *The Hero in Thy Soul,* Chas. Scribner's Sons, 1933.

Hamilton, J. Wallace, "The Deep Roots of Joy," from Hamilton, *Horns and Halos,* Revell, 1954.

Hayward, C. Douglas, "Soul Erosion," from *Pulpit Digest,* July, 1955.

Heuss, John, "Jesus and Our Discouragements," from *Our Christian Vocation,* Seabury Press, 1955.

Hill, Claude E., "Christ and Human Nature," from *The Pulpit*, April, 1948.

Hill, William S., "Life's Foundations," from *The Pulpit*, December, 1952.

Holmes, Kenneth, "A Sermon for Fathers," from *The Pulpit*, June, 1952.

Hope, Norman Vincent, "Christianity—A Layman's Religion," from *Pulpit Digest*, October, 1954.

Horton, Douglas, "Is There Nothing Steadfast in Our World?" from G. Paul Butler, ed., *Best Sermons, 1951-1952*, Macmillan, 1952.

Howard, William Clyde, "How to Love Your Enemies," from *The Pulpit*, February, 1949.

Hudnut, William H., Jr., "On Being Spiritually Prepared for Life," from *The Pulpit*, August, 1949.

Hulme, William, "Run with Patience," from *Pulpit Digest*, March, 1954.

Hunter, Allan A., "Forgive—Or Else," from *The Pulpit*, February, 1946.

Hutchison, Owen, "Jesus and Our Choices," from *The Pulpit*, February, 1956.

Jackson, Edgar N., "And They Lived Happily Ever After," from *Pulpit Digest*, April, 1956.

Jarman, William, "As We See Ourselves," from *The Pulpit*, May, 1944.

Jones, Edgar De Witt, "When Faith Falters," from Jones, *A Man Stood Up to Preach*, Bethany Press, 1943.

Jones, G. Curtis, "On Being Affirmative," from Jones, *On Being Your Best*, Macmillan, 1950.

Jones, John Paul, "For This Time of Tension," from *The Pulpit*, March, 1946.

Jordan, G. Ray, "Living Sanely in an Insane World," from *The Pulpit*, February, 1955.

Kahn, Robert, "Gossip: Major or Minor Sin," from *The Pulpit*, March, 1952.

Kennedy, Gerald, "Cure for Boredom," from *Pulpit Digest*, October, 1955.

Kern, Paul B., "Do We Moderns Need the Man of Galilee?" from *The Pulpit*, April, 1947.

Knapp, William T., "Overcoming Temptation," from *The Pulpit*, September, 1955.

Kolsti, Arthur, Jr., "Homes and the Future," from *The Pulpit*, May, 1953.

Kruener, Harry H., "The Trouble We're In," from *The Pulpit*, August, 1955.

Lemmon, Clarence, "What Are We Working For?" from *The Pulpit*, September, 1948.

Link, James W., "Liking the Hard-to-Like," from *The Pulpit*, February, 1951.

Lorenz, William G., "The Man By the Side of the Road," from *The Pulpit*, September, 1952.

Lowe, Arnold H., "When a Man Looks at Himself," from Lowe, *Start Where You Are*, Harper & Brothers, 1950.

Luccock, Halford H., "Trying to Live on Negatives," from Luccock, *Marching Off the Map*, Harper & Brothers, 1952.

Luccock, Robert, "No Fear of Tomorrow," from Luccock, *If God Be for Us*, Harper & Brothers, 1954.

Lunger, Harold L., "No Place Like Home," from *The Pulpit*, May, 1952.

MacArtney, Clarence, "Life Is Your Battle," from *Pulpit Digest*, December, 1954.

MacLennan, David, "How Can a Man Know God?" from MacLennan, *Joyous Adventure, Sermons for the Christian Year*, Harper & Brothers, 1952.

MacLeod, Donald, "Loneliness—Its Dangers and Its Cure," from *Pulpit Digest*, April, 1955.

McBride, Robert, "The Man Who Grew Up," from *The Pulpit*, July, 1953.

McDowell, Frank K., "You Can't Please Everybody," from *Pulpit Digest*, January, 1954.

Meckel, Aaron N., "What's Wrong With Taking a Drink?" from *Pulpit Digest*, October, 1955.

Meek, Frederick, "Christian Maturity," from *The Pulpit*, February, 1952.

Mendelsohn, S. Felix, "What Can Religion Do for Me?" from *The Pulpit*, March, 1944.

Miller, John H., "Living One Day at a Time," from Miller, *Take a Look at Yourself*, Abingdon-Cokesbury, 1943.

Montgomery, Robert P., "Facing Temptations With God," from *The Pulpit*, January, 1953.

Nelson, J. Robert, "Walls of Hostility," from *The Pulpit*, October, 1955.

Niebuhr, Reinhold, "Sorrow and Joy According to the Christian Faith," from Alton M. Motter, ed., *Great Preaching Today*, Harper & Brothers, 1955.

Nord, Kermit, "How to Be a Bad Parent," from *Pulpit Digest,* April, 1955.

Nyberg, Warren A., "A Cure for Loneliness," from *The Pulpit,* January, 1955.

Oates, Wayne, "The Daily Providence of God," from *Pastoral Psychology,* February, 1955.

Peabody, Stephen, "Managing Our Fears," from *The Pulpit,* May, 1952.

Phillips, Harold Cooke, "Enduring Hardships," from Phillips, *Sails and Anchors,* Judson Press, 1934.

Phillips, J. B., "A God Big Enough," from *Plain Christianity,* The Macmillan Co., 1954.

Pike, James A., "The Best Things in the Worst Times," from G. Paul Butler, ed., *Best Sermons, 1951-1952,* Macmillan Co., 1952.

Pittenger, W. Norman, "Death and the Christian's Attitude Toward It," from *Pulpit Digest,* February, 1956.

Rasmusson, H. Richard, "Building a Home," from *The Pulpit,* May, 1955.

Redhead, John A., Jr., "Christian Self-Love," from *The Pulpit,* August, 1954.

Reid, James, "The Cure of Care," from Reid, *Facing Life With Christ,* Cokesbury, 1940.

Rest, Karl H. A., "The Power of Faith," from *The Pulpit,* March, 1955.

Ruopp, Harold, "Managing Our Tensions and Pressures," from *The Pulpit,* August, 1945.

Russell, Elbert, "Forgetting the Things That Are Behind," from Russell, *A Book of Chapel Talks,* Cokesbury, 1935.

Scherer, Paul E., "Christians in a Non-Christian Society," from *Pulpit Digest,* February, 1954.

Schwarz, L. E., "The Lost Week End," from *The Pulpit,* October, 1946.

Shoemaker, Samuel, "Power to Become," from *Pulpit Digest,* November, 1954.

Sizoo, Joseph, "A Cure for Failure," from Sizoo, *Not Alone,* Macmillan, 1940.

Smith, Charles Merrill, "Why Men Crack Up," from *The Pulpit,* April, 1949.

Smith, Elwyn A., "The Exercise of Charity," from *The Pulpit,* February, 1956.

Stamm, Frederick, "What to Do With Loneliness," from Stamm, *Keeping Men on Their Feet,* Harper & Brothers, 1949.

Straton, Hillyer, "The Problem of My Guilt," from *The Pulpit*, March, 1952.

Swan, Alfred W., "The Christian in His Vocation," from *The Pulpit*, June, 1954.

Tice, Chris, "Resources for the Coming Days," from *Pulpit Digest*, December, 1954.

Trousdale, Whitney, "Roads to a Vital Faith," from *The Pulpit*, March, 1952.

Turner, Herman, "The Christian Home," from *The Pulpit*, May, 1952.

Walker, Alan, "You Are Not Helpless," from *The Pulpit*, March, 1953.

Werner, Hazen G., "You Are Somebody," from Werner, *Real Living Takes Time*, Abingdon, 1948.

Youngdahl, Reuben K., "The Problem of Evil," from *Pulpit Digest*, August, 1956.

Zeller, Harry K., Jr., "Why Do Good People Suffer?" from *The Pulpit*, June, 1954.

APPENDIX II

Biographical Index of Authors

Beaven, Albert (1882-1943), born at Moscow, Idaho. He was educated at Shurtleff College and Rochester Theological Seminary. On graduation from Seminary he became pastor of the Lake Avenue Baptist Church in Rochester, New York, where he had great success as preacher and pastor, but where he was known particularly for developing an effective and well-rounded program for the church. His book *Putting the Church on a Full-Time Basis* told of his program and many of his plans and methods which were widely used in other churches. After twenty years at Lake Avenue Baptist Church he became president of Colgate-Rochester Divinity School, where he also taught in the field of church administration and practical theology. He served for a term as president of the Federal Council (now National Council) of Churches of Christ in America. He also published another volume on church administration, *The Local Church,* two volumes on the home, *The Fine Art of Living Together,* and *Fireside Talks for the Family Circle,* and also books of sermons, *Sermons for Everyday Living* and *The Lift of a Far View.*

Bonnell, John Sutherland (1893-   ). He was born on Prince Edward Island in Canada. He was educated at Dolhausie University, Halifax, Nova Scotia. He served in the Canadian Army in World War I. He served several churches in Canada before he was called to the Fifth Avenue Presbyterian Church in New York City. He has been interested in the relationship of psychology and religion and has lectured on the subject before numerous theological schools. He has published *Pastoral Psychiatry and Psychology for Pastor and People.* He has done much radio preaching, including "National Vespers," each Sunday afternoon. His sermons have appeared in a volume entitled *What Are You Living For?* and in numerous periodicals.

Bowie, Walter Russell (1882-   ). He was born in Richmond,
Virginia, and educated at Harvard University and The Theological Seminary in Virginia. He was rector of Episcopal
churches in Greenwood and Richmond, Virginia, and of Grace
Church in New York City. For eleven years he was professor of practical theology at Union Theological Seminary in
New York, where for five years he served as dean of students.
More recently he has been professor of homiletics at the
Protestant Episcopal Theological Seminary in Virginia. He
is recognized as a biblical scholar, having published several
books on the Bible. His book, *The Story of the Bible,* has
been one of the most popular books in the field. He is an associate editor of the *Interpreter's Bible.* He gave the Yale Lectures on preaching which were published in his book *Preaching.* He has written numerous books of sermons and several
books for young people. His most recent volume is *The Story
of the Church,* a companion volume to *The Story of the Bible.*

Buttrick, George Arthur (1892-   ). He was born in England
but spent all of his ministry in this country. He was educated
in Lancaster Independent College in Manchester and Victoria
University. He served Congregational churches in Illinois and
Vermont, the First Presbyterian Church in Buffalo, and the
Madison Avenue Presbyterian Church in New York City, serving the latter church from 1927 to 1954. He has preached
and lectured before many colleges and universities, including
the Lyman Beecher Lectures at Yale. He is a past president
of the Federal Council of Churches in America and is the
author of numerous books, including *Christian Fact and Modern Doubt, The Parables of Jesus, Prayer, So We Believe So
We Pray, and Faith* and *Education.* He served as editor-in-
chief of the twelve-volume Interpreters' Bible. Since 1955, he
has been on the faculty of Harvard University, where he is
preacher to the University and Plummer Professor of Christian Morals.

Brooks, Phillips (1835-1893). Born at Boston, Mass. Educated
at Harvard and the divinity school in Alexandria, Virginia.
His first pastorate was the Church of the Advent (Episcopal)
in Philadelphia, where he at once proved himself an outstanding preacher. After four years he became rector of Trinity
Church, Boston, where he had amazing success, not only in
his church which he filled to overflowing, but also with the
students at Harvard who came to hear him in great numbers,

and in fact, with people everywhere he went. In 1891 he was chosen Bishop of Massachusetts. He published ten volumes of sermons which still are being read, but is probably best known as the author of the Christmas carol, "O Little Town of Bethlehem." His "Yale Lectures on Preaching" are among the classics in the field of homiletics.

Bushnell, Horace (1802-1876). He was born at Litchfield, Conn. He studied law at Yale and also taught there for a short time. When he came to a conviction for the ministry, he studied theology at Yale. He spent all his ministry in one Congregational church in Hartford, Conn. He is known as a "preacher's preacher," having a tremendous influence on other preachers in America. A versatile writer, he published several volumes of theology, essays, and sermons. His book *Christian Nurture* was perhaps the most influential single volume on religious education in America. He was also very active in civic affairs, working for community betterment, good parks, roads, improvements in government and education.

Finegan, Jack (1908-   ). He was born at Des Moines, Iowa, educated at Drake University and Colgate-Rochester Divinity School. He received his doctoral degree of Lic. theol. *magna cum laude* from the University of Berlin. He was pastor of the First Christian Church, Ames, Iowa. Here, because of his success with students, he was called to the campus of Iowa State College, where he served as director of religious activities and taught courses in philosophy and religion. From Iowa State he went to the Pacific School of Religion, Berkeley, California, where he is head of the Department of Old Testament and New Testament Literature and Interpretation. He also serves as pastor of the First Christian Church at Concord, California. He recently served as a Fulbright Scholar to India. He is recognized as an authority in archeology and has published books and articles in the field. He has also published several books for young people, including *Student Prayers,* a book of answers to youth questions, *Youth Asks About Religion,* and several books of sermons for young people.

Fosdick, Harry Emerson (1878-   ). Born at Buffalo, New York, and educated at Colgate University, Union Theological Seminary, and Columbia University. He was originally a Baptist preacher and his first church was the First Baptist

Church of Montclair, New Jersey. He served for a time as the associate pastor of a Presbyterian Church in New York City but is best known as the pastor of the famous Riverside Church in New York City from 1926 to 1946. While serving as pastor of this church he also served as instructor in homiletics and pastoral theology at Union Theological Seminary. He was a pioneer in radio preaching, one of the first to gain a nation-wide audience. He is the author of twenty-six volumes on a wide variety of subjects. His *The Meaning of Prayer* is accepted as a classic in the devotional life. His Lyman Beecher Lectures at Yale were *The Modern Use of the Bible*. *On Being a Real Person* was on the best-seller lists for a long time. His numerous volumes of sermons have served as patterns for preachers throughout America; in fact, throughout the world.

Jefferson, Charles (1860-1937). He was born at Cambridge, Ohio, educated at Ohio State University. He entered the law school of Boston University but, after coming under the influence of Phillips Brooks, transferred to the Divinity School. He served for ten years as pastor of the Central Congregational Church, Chelsea, Mass. From there he went to Broadway Tabernacle, in New York City, which is known as "the skyscraper church." He had a long and significant ministry in this church in the heart of New York City for more than thirty years. He is perhaps best known as the author of four small volumes on the ministry, *The Minister as Shepherd, The Minister as Prophet, The Building of the Church*, which was the Yale Lectures in 1910, and *Quiet Hints to Growing Preachers*. He also published several volumes of sermons. His books of sermons often included a series he had preached, such as "Nature Sermons," "The Character of Paul," "The Character of Jesus."

McCracken, Robert (1904-   ). He was born in Scotland and educated in Edinburgh and Glasgow. He held pastorates in Edinburgh and Glasgow before coming to Canada where he taught Christian theology and philosophy at McMaster University for eight years. He was called by Riverside Church in New York City to succeed Dr. Harry Emerson Fosdick as pastor of this famous church. Here he very rapidly came into prominence as a preacher in his own right. He has published one volume of sermons, *Questions People Ask,* and one book on preaching, *The Making of the Sermon.*

Sockman, Ralph W. (1889-   ). He was born in Mount Vernon, Ohio, and educated at Ohio Wesleyan, Union Theological Seminary and Columbia University, where he received his Ph.D. degree. He has spent his entire ministry at Christ Methodist Church in New York City. A very popular preacher, he has gained a nationwide audience as preacher over a national radio network. A frequent lecturer before colleges and theological seminaries, he has also published many books, thus furthering his influence. He gave the Lyman Beecher Lectures at Yale in 1941, *The Highway of God.* He has published several volumes of sermons, *Live for Tomorrow, Date with Destiny, Now to Live* and others.

Weatherhead, Leslie (1893-   ). He was born in London, educated at London University, Manchester University, and Richmond Hill Theological College. He served in the British Army in World War I, first as an officer of the line and later as a chaplain. He served as the pastor of the English Methodist Church in Madras, India, as pastor of the Methodist Church in Manchester and in Leeds. Since 1936 he has been pastor of City Temple in London. A student of psychology, he has utilized it in his own work, conducting a psychological clinic in relationship with his church. A prolific writer, he has written primarily in two fields—the relationship of psychology and religion, and books of sermons. Among the first group are *Psychology in the Service of the Soul,* one of the early volumes, and *Psychology, Religion and Healing,* his most comprehensive. His books of sermons often follow a biblical theme, such as *Personalities of the Passion* (biblical personalities) and *In Quest of a Kingdom* (sermons from the parables). Some of his books of sermons deal with general subjects, such as *The Significance of Silence,* and other volumes.